THE
OCCULT EXPERIENCE
PROOF OF THE PARANORMAL

JOHN KREITER

The Occult Experience

Copyright © 2013 John Kreiter

www.johnkreiter.com

All rights reserved. No part of this book shall be reproduced, stored in a retrieval system, or transmitted by any means—electronic, mechanical, photocopying, recording, or otherwise—without written permission from the publisher, except for the inclusion of brief quotations in a review.

Authors and the publisher shall have neither liability nor responsibility to any person or entity with respect to any loss or damages arising from the information contained in this book.

TABLE OF CONTENTS

Forword 1
CHAPTER 1 The Mad Logician 7
CHAPTER 2 The Sensual Deception 21
CHAPTER 3 The Mob Rules 35
CHAPTER 4 The Doing of Not Doing 51
CHAPTER 5 Seeing Auras / Energetic Perception ... 65
CHAPTER 6 Breaking the Biggest Routine of All 79
CHAPTER 7 The Power of Beliefs 95
CHAPTER 8 A road Sign to High Strangeness 105
CHAPTER 9 The Proper Use of Banishment 117
Epilogue 135
Further Reading 141

FORWORD

This book is written for those that would like to expand their sense perceptions. It is a collection of ideas and methodologies that will allow you to expand your capabilities and greatly increase your sensual and intuitive perceptions. It will allow you to perceive the paranormal world around you. It is ideal for those that want to explore the paranormal 'out there'. It is a book that is designed to prove to you, if you're willing to make the effort and work on the exercises given, that reality is far more than the solid and mechanical world that you might currently see before you. The methods described in this book will take you as far as you wish to go; you can use them to see more and experience more, you can use them to greatly increase your ability to research the paranormal, you can use them to completely dissolve your idea of what reality really is, you can use them to gain personal power over your environment, or you can use them to get lost in the infinity that is all around us. Correct use of correct knowledge is power.

In the first chapter we are introduced to logic, empirical evidence, and the power of assumptions. We lightly touch upon the incredible importance of beliefs and how they are a key factor in creating our perceptive reality. We discuss our mad logician and his inability to live in either the past or the future because of his inability to make assumptions. I do hope that you look deeply into this chapter because there's a lot more being said here than you might first realize. This chapter will allow you to see the crux of the mistake that we are making in our modern society when it comes to temporal awareness and dogmatic belief structures. In this chapter you will discover the logical basis for a temporally different type of awareness. This awareness-structure has become popular lately in the West but has been a part of Asian thought for thousands of years, you can find it in; Zen, Ch'an, Taoism, Buddhism.

In Chapters 2 and 3 we begin to look into the idea of cognitive conditioning. We begin in Chapter 2 by considering some interesting illusions in order to demonstrate how our senses have evolved and how this evolution has given us certain advantages and limitations. We consider the possibility that seemingly hardwired visual characteristics might be far more flexible than we imagine. In Chapter 3 we continue this by exploring how these cognitive viewpoints can be changed through beliefs. We introduced the concept of memes and take a deeper look into the incredibly powerful indoctrination system that we all experience from the moment of our birth.

In Chapter 4 we begin to practice methodologies in order to break our cognitive conditioning. I give you background on why these exercises were developed and I give you a good selection of exercises that you can practice on your own. These are very powerful exercises that will allow you to begin to see the world from a different angle and as such will completely alter the way that you perceive the world around you. These exercises are not a joke and they must be treated with respect by anyone who is prepared to practice them on a regular basis.

Chapter 5 begins your journey into real practical application. In this chapter you learn about the possibilities of extending your visual perceptions and how to begin to see a little more of that amazing world 'out there'. Here I show you real practical techniques in order to see frequencies that are supposedly outside of our visual perception. I teach you how to see what is colloquially referred to as Auras and how to sense the subtler energy all around you.

Using the methods in Chapter 6, you should begin to tap directly into the subconscious. This is an incredibly vast universe, this subconscious realm, which is far more complex than what we consider normal waking reality. Training your awareness to stay awake as it were during your sleep phase, will allow you to begin to explore this vast universe; a universe that could take a civilization centuries or perhaps millennia to explore. But you can begin this quest on your own to a satisfactory degree using this methodology. Beyond this, these methods will allow you to perceive what is referred to as alien energy in this field of reality, this vast subconscious. This is perhaps the ultimate way to expand our capabilities into what could literally be termed other dimensions.

Chapter 7 is the straw that broke the camel's back. If you have been practicing all of the exercises and have been conceptualizing deeply the ideas and methodologies mentioned up to this point, Chapter 7 is most likely the chapter that could drive you literally over the edge. Now I don't want to drive you insane, but sanity my friends is not all it's cracked up to be (is there a pun in that?). Using the methods in this chapter, you will begin to make some deep psychological changes. These changes might actually start to reconstruct some of your neurological patterning and will, facilitate to a great degree, your extrasensory perceptions. Please do not be afraid of this since any methodology can always be terminated if you find it to be too much for you.

But I do hope that you push yourself using the exercises in this chapter. Doing so will put you on a greater edge and allow you to expand your capabilities to an incredible degree.

Think of Chapter 8 as fair warning. Not a warning asking you to keep out, but more as a signal in the road letting you know what will be coming up ahead so that you are prepared.

Chapter 9 on the other hand is the chapter where you are given your bronze shield, which is the final thing that you will need on your journey.

If you are ready to begin then let's begin at the beginning…

CHAPTER 1
THE MAD LOGICIAN

The world does not exist the way we think it does. I am certain that you have heard this statement many times. It is an idea that has been explored at great length and it seems to be verified both scientifically and psychologically. But what does this mean?

Perhaps, if you are interested in the subject, you have seen or heard a number sources talk about the limitations of our perceptual senses. For nearly a century now we have known that everything that we see around us, including ourselves, is made up of atoms. As we know from science class, these atoms are essentially vibrating energy and as a result we must conclude that we too are not the material creatures that we imagine. According to these theories, we must begin to accept as reality the fact that we are essentially vibrating energy and, in many ways, as insubstantial as a wisp of smoke.

> *The funny thing is that while science can say that it has verified to its own conclusion, that indeed we are far less substantial than we imagine, these same truths have been advocated by mystics and ancient schools of thought for thousands of years. If these old dogmas are now considered our reality by modern science, what other ancient ideas might be true as well?*

We love to stick to our old routines. We don't want to hear that things are not the way they seem because we are quite comfortable thank you very much. Plus, how on earth does it help us in any way to know that we are insubstantial things. It certainly won't change the way of the world, will it? And if it does, wouldn't these revelations and their possible consequence cast us into a sea of insanity and chaos?

Philosophers have also believed for a very long time that our interpretation of the reality around us is incorrect. Most philosophy is based on the idea that our sensual data and the way that we choose to define our existence is wrong. Philosophers have taken it for granted that our senses do not function as well as we would like them to and have tried to redefine the terms of our existence through thought and internal questioning.

As science took hold of the human psyche and stepped out of its shaky beginnings, it too began to conclude as follows; that our senses are not telling us the truth, at least they're not giving us the full picture. With such thoughts in mind, that man and his senses are essentially flawed and that the only way to really understand reality is to focus on empirical measures and ideas, the priests of science went about creating tools and dogmas that would completely change the way we view reality.

There was one particular innovation by philosophers that science found quite interesting. It was a discipline that was always intertwined with what would eventually become formal science; this was the discipline of **logic**.

Here is a dictionary definition of logic (dictionary.reference.com):

1. The science that investigates the principles governing correct or reliable inference.

2. A particular method of reasoning or argumentation: We were unable to follow his logic.

3. The system or principles of reasoning applicable to any branch of knowledge or study.

4. Reason or sound judgment, as in utterances or actions: There wasn't much logic in her move.

5. Convincing forcefulness; inexorable truth or persuasiveness: the irresistible logic of the facts.

If you look at these definitions, you get a basic idea of what logic is all about. It is essentially a way to know the truthfulness or the fallacy of any particular argument. It can be quite simple and also quite complex depending on the complexity of the content that you are trying to study.

In my opinion the best way to think about logic is to think of it like this;

I know that this is so because of that, where that has been proven empirically.

In this way we are able to understand greater truths, using empirical evidence sort of like a mental scaffolding. We can gain greater understanding of far more complex and harder to understand possibilities by logically structuring and verifying complex ideas.

Name any science that you care to think of; chemistry, biology, physics, etc. Realize that they are all built upon logical mental scaffolding. Science has used these logical methods to expand its understanding of many of the mysteries that surround us. And logic as a general science, in and of itself, is the basis for most of our modern computational technology. All of our computational software and much of our computational electrical hardware works on the principle of yes or no, the 0 or 1.

Now my desire is not to get into complex logical theory because this book is not about logical theory but about the expansion of personal perception and capability. If you wish to study logic there are many wonderful books out there that will open your eyes to this magnificent science/philosophy. But why then do I bring this subject to light in the very first chapter of the book?

It is because through some personal introspection, backed up by good logical methodology, we can begin to understand the true fallacy of our external perceptions. In order to expand our perceptions and begin to experience a greater reality and capability, we first need to prove to ourselves that what we are seeing 'out there' is quite limited and often times quite wrong.

Using the very logic that is most often brought up by the skeptic[1], we can begin to realize that our perception of external reality is quite limited and flawed. Beyond this we can begin to discover that much of what we believe to be 'out there' is really a type of mass mental indoctrination. An indoctrination that tells us that the world is a concrete and mechanical place and it has very little room for spirits, UFOs, psychic ability, monsters, or anything that is currently called the paranormal.

Now before we get into questioning our current sensual perceptions, I want to share with you a

---

[1] By the way, the zealot skeptic sucks at logic. If he were actually able to maneuver within its depths, instead of just quoting supposed logical conclusions, he could never maintain his skeptical zealousness.

personal definition that I find very helpful; and this is the difference between logic and reasoning:

- I define logic as what is stated above and whatever you discover in your personal study of logic.

- But reasoning on the other hand, I define as the act of making assumptions.

Now if you are a student of logic then you might want to string me up for any kind of definition as such. You would most likely let me know right away that any kind of logical progression needs to make certain assumptions as long as that which came before, the content of the material, can be proven to be a non-fallacy.

If this is what you would tell me, then I would agree with you 100%. But if we were to look at things in a truly logical fashion, you would discover that there are many things that are assumed to be true without the proof that is necessary to justify them. The proof provided is usually that of scientists working somewhere, and their conclusions. But unless you can replicate those conclusions yourself or can prove that these conclusions can be replicated beyond a shadow of doubt under any circumstance or location, you are making an assumption. Scientists, believe it or not, make mistakes; they also lie, cheat, and cook data if the grant is big enough. Just because a guy with a scientist badge said so doesn't mean it's real; science after all is not supposed to be a religion and 'scientists' are not clergy. I am not saying that scientific data is questionable, what I am saying is that all data should be questioned. Assumption, ANY assumption, is the mother of all screw-ups.

My definition of logic therefore is a far more flexible methodology, not in that things can come from nowhere and be allowed to be true. But in the fact that I believe that logic can be far more flexible in its ability to understand things from different perspectives. That is, logical progression can come about through a number of different data streams, can take different paths, and come to different conclusions depending on how this data is perceived. The 'perception' here is reasoning and as I have defined above; reasoning is essentially, an act of assumption.

Current 'normal' human perception can only occur through assumption

As an example, let us take a very hot topic; let's consider the idea of God:

A monotheistic religion like Christianity believes that there is one God in heaven who is responsible for all creation and that God must be worshiped.

Atheistic thought believes that there is no God, or greater deities, and that the world is a mechanistic creation brought about by measurable laws that can explain both its past and its future.

Know which is true? The interesting thing is that you can use logic to prove either one and the only difference between either is where you make an assumption.

Now while many a scientifically minded individual or skeptic might tell you that logic will essentially prove them to be correct, that God does not exist, this is not the case. Logic can prove either Christianity or Atheism to be correct because there is always a point where an assumption is made that cannot be proven beyond doubt. Notice that I did not say 'proven empirically'.

Empirically is defined as (thefreedictionary.com):

1.
    a. Relying on or derived from observation or experiment: *empirical results that supported the hypothesis.*
    b. Verifiable or provable by means of observation or experiment: *empirical laws.*
2. Guided by practical experience and not theory.

So far so good says the atheist but perhaps he shouldn't get so comfortable. Since this seems to be his bread-and-butter, the atheist will tell you about study upon study done to prove his point of view. And with great passion might begin to inform us that while his conclusions are based on empirical evidence, any conclusion made by the religionist is not. But our friend the atheist should perhaps reread the definition of what empirical means.

Certainly, the atheist's assumption, that God is not real, is based on logical methodology. If he knows his stuff, he can quote any number of studies and experiments to prove his point. Indeed, since science has taken such a great hold of the human psyche, he is definitely in good footing here in our current era. But what the atheist does not consider is the fact that there is a great deal of empirical evidence to prove the existence of God as well.

> *If what we know about ancient Hebrew culture is correct, then it is easy to see that those that lay the foundation for Christianity were highly adept individuals. People that experienced monumental perceptions, perceptions that were well documented. We can also see that certain experiments were done and that through these experiments they were able to discover a methodology that allowed them to have a far more direct communication with something they called God. These methodologies were experienced over and over again and the success of Christianity, its ability to be able to change the mass psyche of the times, was proof of the power of their logical conclusions.*

Logically speaking both the atheist and the religionist are correct, to the point that they are both willing to make an assumption that they both believe is empirically correct. What both these points of view suffer from is really a type of snobbery. What the atheist believes and what the religionist believes are both based on empirical evidence in that they are both based on experimental, observable, practical data. They are snobs because neither wishes to believe that the practical work, perceptions, and experiments of the other are valid. Essentially, they are both fighting over an assumption.

Assumption = Belief

Atheists might tell you that they are not making assumptions but only working on a probable theory, which is what science does, but the reality is that those theories are never presented as theories but as facts instead.

> *When truly pressed about their methodology, a scientist will tell you that he or she is only speaking of the latest and best theory or model; that these theories, or the models that they are currently using, is always up for revision if differing verifiable data becomes available. But:*
>
> - *try telling a scientist in 1794 (when Ernst Chladni published the idea that meteorites were rocks from space) that rocks could fall from the sky, or*

> - *an astrophysicist 20 years ago that there are 'many' planets outside the solar system that can support life.*
>
> *Either one of these things could get you in deep trouble at the time.*
>
> *If you don't believe that the scientific establishment has the power to destroy then look up what happened to Wilhelm Reich.*

The atheist believes that the scientific and empirical work done by those that he believes in, is correct and beyond question. He does not question the fact that those that believe what he believes, perhaps the majority of the scientific community, have never actually performed any real 'empirical' experimentation into the possibility of the existence of God. Even though Heisenberg's uncertainty principle lets us know that there is no possibility of observing something without affecting it, the atheist seldom considers the possibility that an atheist trying to find God is sort of like a fish trying to find water.

The Christian of course is in exactly the same place. He does not question the empirical data that was gathered by individuals that died thousands of years ago. For him it is blasphemy to even postulate the idea that some of this empirical data might be interpreted incorrectly, that some of this data might be incorrect, or perhaps even tampered with. The

Atheist is unholy, deluded, and depending on what Christian you talk to, evil.

Neither the Christian nor the atheist will question his sources to a great degree. Neither will question the idea that an assumption (the individual came to a reasonable conclusion) was made and that this assumption might be wrong. Fundamentally it comes down to the ego, and the ego is a master at hiding lies and half-truths.

But what conclusions are we to come to then if we can come to no conclusions? What kind of life will we have if we can't have facts to make us feel cozy and safe? Is it really possible to live without beliefs? Or is perhaps the belief that there are no beliefs a type of belief?

> *What if we try to think of things logically without coming to any reasonable conclusion all? What are we left with?*
>
> *What we are fundamentally left with is that our entire perceptive capability is based on our five senses. Anything beyond current perception in the present moment (using my idea of logic) is an assumption and therefore cannot be logically trusted.*
>
> *You see if logical reasoning is used on past data, then this data is an assumption. For example, let's say that you are walking down the street and*

walk by a mailbox, as you pass by the mailbox you are not currently looking at it but have a memory of it and as such you can conclude that there is a mailbox just behind you. This is a conclusion that we all take for granted and a good memory is indeed a positive trait. But if we are to look at things in a purely logical fashion, then we cannot assume anything and therefore we cannot assume that there is a mailbox behind us. Indeed, how many times have you made a mistake where you think you have seen a certain thing but turning around to look at it again you discover that it was something altogether different?

Logic without any reasonable assumptions then tells us that the only thing that exists is what we can perceive in the present moment. The past and the future are a fallacy and as such the mind is a fallacy as well. Beyond this, things outside of our perceptive abilities are also a type of fallacy because trying to rationalize what they are is a fallacy for this type of logic. We cannot see what is behind a wall or hear what is beyond the range of our hearing; anything beyond our senses does not exist.

A logician without reason cannot be a Christian because heaven is in the future and he cannot be an atheist either because he certainly cannot conclude on any kind of data from the past, data that he probably didn't even have any direct involvement in gathering anyway. The only thing that our mad logician can do is to perceive the present moment, and the funny thing about the present moment is that assumptions are an impossibility.

POINTS TO REMEMBER:

- Logic is far more flexible than most people realize because with it you can explain any number of possible conclusions.
- Logic is flexible because it relies on empirical evidence.
- Empirical evidence is not truth but perception that is shared by many individuals.
- Perception is directly related to reasoning where reasoning is defined as the act of making assumptions.
- Everything is an assumption because nothing can be known with 100% certainty.
- Assumption equals belief.
- Depending on your beliefs you can either be a Christian, an Atheist, a Hindu, a Satanist, or an insane logician.
- Beliefs are VERY important.
- In order to begin to expand your senses and capabilities, you must begin to focus your attention on the present moment because it's the only place free of assumption!

CHAPTER 2
THE SENSUAL DECEPTION

Our senses lie. They're not trying to be mean and they're not trying to delude us per se, our senses lie because some part of us, a long time ago, decided that seeing things in a certain way was preferable.

Our senses lie to us and they also give us a really limited perspective of the world in which we exist. This is a very important thing to understand if we wish to expand our perceptions and therefore increase our capability as human beings. It is important because by realizing that our current perceptions are mistaken, we can become aware of the fact that even within our limited perception, there is the possibility of seeing the world in a completely different way than the one that we are used to. It is also important because we must realize that our senses have a very limited range and it is therefore quite possible, and indeed the case, that there is a lot going on around us that we are completely unaware of.

Let us contemplate the most important sense that we have, our vision:

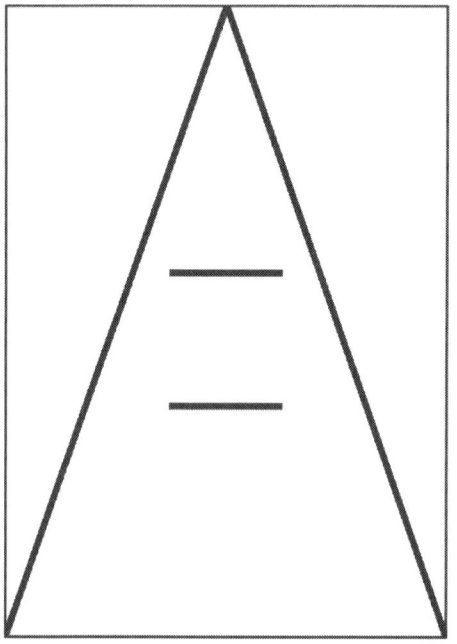

Figure 1. Ponzo Illusion

The above image is a good representation of how our eyes lie to us. The two horizontal lines are of equal length but the vertical lines create a false sense of perspective which makes us believe that the higher of the two horizontal lines is longer. This is false perspective and allows us to instantly know whether something is close to us or really far away.

Figure 2. Kanizsa's Triangle
https://commons.wikimedia.org/wiki/File:Kanizsa_triangle.svg

The above images are called the Kanizsa's Triangles after the Italian psychologist who invented them, Gaetano Kanizsa. Can you see the white triangle? The white triangle is called subjective contour and our eyes easily see this triangle as if it were real. It is actually very hard, and for some people it's impossible, to 'not' see the triangles.

Figure 3. Depth spheres

The above images create the illusion of depth or indentation depending on where the light source is perceived. The shading in and of itself creates an illusion that tricks our eyes into thinking that there is greater depth than there really exists. Furthermore, the perception of light coming from below makes us believe that there is an indentation instead of a protrusion.

These images are a simple example of how the eye goes about deceiving us, fooling us into believing an interpretation of what is out there instead of the actual data that we know to exist in reality. Evolutionary anthropologists believe that these perceptual illusions became hardwired into our system in order to help us function with greater ability in our world. For example, the depth of field illusion allows us to see a predator or prey and instantly judge its distance from us using only minimal cues. This ability would seem essential when seconds count and we really don't have any time to think, but only to act.

But are these perceptual irregularities really hardwired into our system? And if they are, can we control or override them in any way?

The anthropologist Colin Turnbull studied the pygmies in the Congo and was able to discover some amazing things about human perception. Turnbull discovered that because the pygmies live their entire lives in the forest, they were not able to judge the size of objects properly because of the fact that they had never had a chance to look at something that was a long distance away from them.

He relates a tale of how he once took his Pygmy guide Kenge out of the forest in into an open field. He writes, "Kenge looked over the plane and down to a herd of buffalo some miles away. He asked me what kind of insects they were, and I told him Buffalo, twice as big as the forest buffalo known to him. He laughed loudly and told me not to tell him such stupid stories... We got into the car and drove down to where the animals were grazing. He watched them getting larger and larger, and even though he was as courageous as any pygmy, he moved over and sat close to me and muttered that it was witchcraft. When he realized they were real buffalo he was no longer afraid, but what puzzled him was why they had been so small, and whether they had really been small and suddenly grown larger or whether it had been some kind of trickery." (Turnbull 1963, 217)

Another group of interesting people are the Piraha people of the Amazon. They are incredibly well-suited for their environment and it is said that they could walk naked into the jungle and get for themselves every single thing that they could possibly want in order to survive and thrive in their environment. Interestingly though it seems that these people are not able to count beyond the number five. Their language has no words for precise numbers but rather a concept for smaller and larger amounts.

This interesting cultural peculiarity shows that the Piraha have no need or desire for any kind of counting and therefore have no perceptual way to separate large quantities of individual units. It is a good example of the fact that human perception is far more flexible than we currently believe it is. Indeed, studies into the perceptual differences of feral children, children that have lived completely in the wild and away from any kind of civilized indoctrination, shows us that much of our cognitive functioning is a learnt response.

Earlier we touched upon the fact that scientists had discovered what ancient mystics and mystery schools have been saying for a long time; that the world that we see through our senses is not the world that really exists 'out there'. The cognitive studies mentioned above indicate that our perception is in some ways far more skewed than just the inability to see our vibrational nature. Scientists seem to be in a game of catch-up right now, perhaps one day they will come up with an interpretation that fundamentally completely agrees with these old schools of thought.

So, what do these schools of thought tell us about the reality of our perception? Perhaps this can help us to get a head start on the current scientific community; most often times skeptic community, so that we can begin to take steps to expand our reality.

Sorcerers, Shaman, magicians, witch doctors, ancient schools of secret knowledge, have been telling their disciples for thousands of years that the world that we see out there is only there because of a systematic indoctrination. This indoctrination is carried out by every single human being that we come across, and together we all work towards creating a stable perceptual reality that we can all share.

They tell us that while this perceptual reality that we all work to create has many advantages, it also has many limitations. It allows us to function as a community and species, in a predatory world. This perceptual reality has allowed us to dominate our environment for the most part and has allowed us to interact as a community; giving all of us the ability to share and interact with each other.

For example, let's say that we are both looking at a certain house plant. I take it for granted that we are both looking at a plant because we choose to agree on the fact that the shared perceptions in a certain space and time denote a plant. It is not the case that I am seeing what you are seeing because from my point in space and time I am not seeing the same thing as you. But I can agree with you that we are looking at the same thing through different cognitive cues that we have agreed on as a species. The importance of this ability cannot be overestimated; without it our civilization would be possible.

Unfortunately, this learnt 'cognitive cooperation' has also created many perceptual failures. The 'old schools' tell us that our learnt 'cognitive slant' does not allow us to see the great marvel of the universe around us. It makes us believe that life is simple and mechanical (a world made up of objects), but that in reality life is made up of infinitely mysterious events. They tell us that if the average man were to see a more accurate version of reality, he would most likely go temporarily mad because of the great marvels that exist just beyond our perceptual reach. Actually, a good definition of insanity is the inability of an individual to operate on the same cognitive structure as the cognitive structure used by all of the individuals around him.

THE KING AND THE POISONED WELL

There was once a wise king who ruled over a vast kingdom. He was feared for his might and loved for his wisdom. Now in the heart of the city, there was a well with pure water from which the king and all the people of the kingdom drank. When all were asleep, a witch entered the city and poured seven drops of a strange liquid into the well. She said that henceforth all who drink this water shall become mad.

The next day, all the people drank of the water, but not the king. And the people began to say, "The king is mad and has lost his reason. Look how strangely he behaves. We cannot be ruled by a madman, so he must be dethroned."

The king grew very fearful, for his subjects were preparing to rise against him. That evening, he ordered a golden goblet to be filled from the well, and he drank deeply. The next day, there was great rejoicing among the people, for their beloved king had finally regained his reason.

— Author Unknown

The old schools believe that it's taken a lifetime of individual existence to teach us how to see the world in the right way and it can therefore take a lifetime to re-teach us to see the world in a way that is slightly closer to its fundamental reality. The old schools tend to believe that the average cognitive system is a type of slavery and that it is up to them to redefine cognitive awareness for their disciples because it is only through this redefinition that their disciples are able to become adepts.

Why do these old schools go to so much trouble? Why is it so important that its disciples realign their cognitive perceptions? Is it a type of brainwashing?

Certainly, in a general sense, any kind of cognitive re-adjustment is a type of brainwashing. This cognitive realignment will most likely create adepts that are completely devoted to the organization that has changed their reality. This devotion is after all critical in the survival of any particular secret society, making sure that this knowledge and power continues into the next generation.

But there is more to it than that. Social scientists will tell you that most of these old schools gain(ed) their power through communal organizations that excluded anyone not of that tradition. They refer to the priesthoods of a certain religions or the collusion of secret organizations such as the Freemasons.

Again, I'm certain that this was and is the case in many of these secretive organizations but that is not the whole truth. The reality is that many individuals wanted to become members of these old schools, especially the more ancient ones like Shamanism, because they knew that there was great perceptual power to be gained by becoming a member. People join the schools readily because they wish to gain power. Increased cognitive ability creates more possibility and this possibility can be used to gain wealth, recognition, and generally a greater ability to thrive. We must also not forget that many would join such organizations because of a thirst for knowledge; this after all is an inherent trait of our species.

Science as we have noted has a hard time admitting that a world exists beyond its understanding. Its belief system is such that it can only see power gained through collusion and social control, at this time it cannot begin to postulate the possibility that humanity has far greater capabilities than most scientists now presuppose.

The below figure is a representation of the electromagnetic spectrum. The electromagnetic spectrum is the range of all possible frequencies of electromagnetic radiation (Wikipedia). Of all of the possible radiation that can exist all around you at this moment, our eyes can only perceive that tiny little slit worth of radiation indicated below.

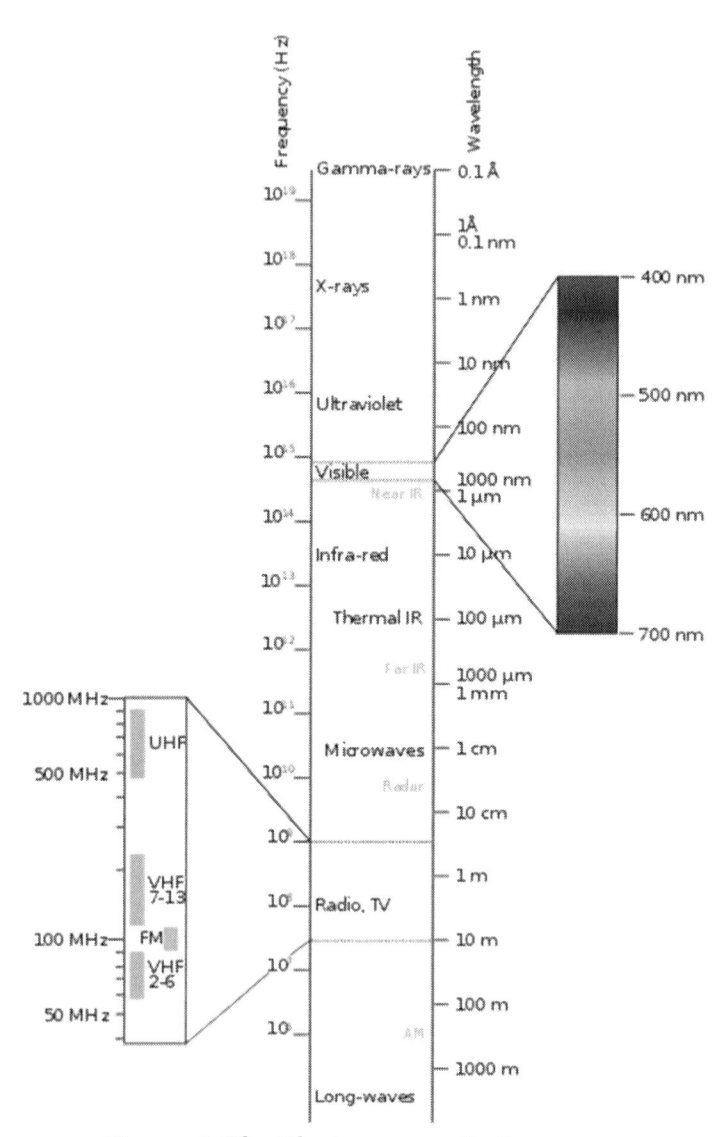

Figure 4. The Electromagnetic Spectrum
https://commons.wikimedia.org/wiki/File:Electromagnetic-Spectrum.svg

The next time that a person tells you that ghosts, UFOs, or any of the other paranormal things that some have reported seeing cannot exist, perhaps you should show him or her this chart. Imagine how utterly simplistic it is to believe that things do not exist because we cannot see them while all around us there is a HUGE amount of electromagnetic radiation, a far greater universe of available data, that we '*supposedly*' cannot perceive at all.

As you look around your room or wherever you might find yourself at the moment, it is quite possible that there is something quite close to you right now that would blow your mind if your vision could perceive just a little more of the electromagnetic spectrum.

Well it seems that our understanding of the world around us is constantly changing. The scientific community is constantly revising what it believes to be possible as it expands its understanding of the physical universe. Perhaps science one day will discover the fact that our cognitive system can be changed considerably and perhaps through this change in beliefs, new perceptive abilities will become possible.

Remember that before the 1800s rocks couldn't fall from the sky... but now they do and we call them meteorites.

POINTS TO REMEMBER:

- Our senses are lying to us.

- Our senses aren't evil; it is just that we decided some time back that things worked much better using our current cognitive slant.

- The old schools have told us this for perhaps thousands of years.

- The old schools believed that they could retrain the human cognitive system in order to expand awareness.

- Science in some ways is playing catch-up with these old schools of thought. It doesn't believe it, but it is.

- People that tell you that the paranormal is not real because they can't see it have very little understanding of the vastness of what is out there. Perhaps you should carry a graph of the electromagnetic spectrum in your pocket.

- Our current cognitive slant is hugely dependent on socialization and learnt behavior. Change that behavior and you literally change the world...But never forget the story of the king and the well.

CHAPTER 3
THE MOB RULES

So how do we know what we know?

Perhaps we look out and see a certain thing and through this sense perception we begin to believe that there is something 'out there'. We stretch out our arms and feel this, perhaps, furry object and begin to take it for granted that what we are looking at is 'real'.

But what if someone comes along and looks where we are looking and waves his hands where we were touching and says that there is nothing there at all. "No Billy I do not see a giant furry six-foot pink bunny rabbit."

And that's basically it!

That is how we come to most of our perceptual conclusions. Using our senses, we perceive certain data, we perform experiments on this data and we wait to see if others get the same results that we do. If enough people agree that there is indeed a 6 foot tall pink bunny rabbit then the 6 foot tall pink bunny rabbit is real. If we see this 6 foot tall pink bunny rabbit and insist that it is there even though no one else can see it, then we are shipped off to a loony bin and doctors either 'fix' us or we are sequestered somewhere, kept far away from normal people so that we do not scare them with our 'unreasonable' perceptions.

> *If you ever get really tired of watching Jimmy Stewart in "It's a Wonderful Life" during the Christmas season, then might I suggest that you try and get yourself a copy of "Harvey" instead.*

Because there was always someone that came before you, most of this cognitive experimentation has already been done. From the moment that you become aware, every person in your life begins to define the world around you. As a baby, your mom might say, "Look Billy you're on a chair. This is a chair isn't it hard? What a beautiful chair, can you say chair? Yes, you can say chair...boga boga boga!"

As you progress in years, you begin to define the reality before you and, in this way, begin to understand and become able to communicate with those around you. You are told that no there is no monster in your closet and no there is no Santa Claus either, but if you put your hand on the fire you will get burned[2].

> *If we take it for granted that telepathic communication does exist, then we must conclude that this cognitive conditioning might even begin before we are born (while we are conscious in the womb), while we sleep, and for the rest of our lives whether we are aware of it or not.*
>
> *So, you think telepathy is not real? Well you should definitely not tell 'the hundredth monkey' that. It is also very important that you do not Google why most scientific drug experiments need to use a procedure called 'double-blind'. But whatever you do, stay away from Carl Jung' unconscious (collective or otherwise), Rupert Sheldrake, and Joseph Banks Rhine.*

Even without the belief in telepathy, this mass human indoctrination is actually incredibly complex and all encompassing. It may begin with simple things like the ability to name an object and define its boundaries, but quickly gets far more complex. Since our beliefs are so important, there is also a conscious

---

[2] Victor, a feral boy that was picked up by farmers at the edge of a village in southern France, was said to be able to pluck potatoes from a boiling kettle without being burnt. It is said that he would show no discomfort during the winter months and had no use for fire.

and an unconscious desire and demand in society to control these beliefs and to disseminate/allow only those beliefs that seem advantageous at the time.

The study of the meme[3], has given us great insight into the ability of an idea, behavior, or style to be passed on to others. Through this study we have been able to see how these infectious ideas can dictate human action and perception. A meme can be as small as a hand gesture or as large as a global religious movement. The human desire to perpetuate a meme and to become part of a collective unit (or mob) is amazing.

These memes seem to somehow become live entities that feed off of the attention and energy that is given off by its believers. Another way to see these memes is to see them as a type of weather pattern affecting different parts of the Earth, clashing into each other, and creating complex chaotic (like math) systems. And as difficult as it is to forecast a weather pattern, it is indeed far more difficult to forecast the

---

[3] A **meme** is "an idea, behavior or style that spreads from person to person within a culture." A meme acts as a unit for carrying cultural ideas, symbols or practices, which can be transmitted from one mind to another through writing, speech, gestures, rituals or other imitable phenomena. Supporters of the concept regard memes as cultural analogues to genes in that they self-replicate, mutate and respond to selective pressures. Source: Wikipedia/Merriam-Webster Dictionary/Graham, Gordon (2002), *Genes: a philosophical inquiry*, New York: Routledge, p. 196

consequences brought about by a very powerful meme.

We do not need to study these complex chaotic systems, but it is essential that we understand how completely these systems affect us and the people around us. Contemplation of these systems will allow you to see the grand structure that is responsible for the collective human psyche. This psyche as I said has many advantageous properties but at the same time has many disadvantages as well. The disadvantage that we are most concerned with here is that they create many limitations upon those that are a part of the system. When you are part of the system you are essentially stuck in a 'matrix', just like the movie, where you believe the notion that the world exists in only one way. Anyone who steps outside of this belief system, this collective human belief, is in danger of being ostracized and quite possibly killed.

> *Again, if you do not believe that a meme can kill you then all you need to do is look back in history at the many movements (memes) that have taken root and have made any kind of major change in human society. Think about the witch trials, Christianity, communism, or capitalism for example, and how many individuals were tortured and killed in the name of a belief.*

But like I said we do not need to get too complex, we just need to understand how it works and how it is that this type of indoctrinated belief structure limits our potential perceptive capabilities. Let's contemplate a simple example;

Think back to a time when you were just beginning school, you were in kindergarten and you had just started school for the first time. Perhaps during this time, like many children, you had an imaginary friend. Now in kindergarten this is not a major problem. It is quite possible that the kid taking a nap next to you had such an imaginary friend also.

Many children have this kind of pretend friend or seem to easily see things that are considered to be the work of a healthy childish imagination. But think about the connotations of the word 'childish', how this word describes exactly how the rest of the world sees this perceptual oddity, the ability to interact with objects that are considered to be insubstantial, invisible, or imaginary to the rest of the people around you. Most likely your parents put up with your adventurous imagination for a while, but around this time they are beginning to curtail this imagination by having you understand that there are many things 'out there' that don't exist like you think they do.

Perhaps your teachers in kindergarten are also letting you know that it is healthy to have an imaginary friend but that it's a lot better to play with 'real' kids. You are being told over and over again that the big 6 foot tall pink bunny rabbit is not real. This collective meme; the idea that illusory mental projections (or otherwise) are not healthy and cannot exist, is believed and exercised by all the grownups around you. You are given a certain amount of time, childhood, in which you can begin to become part of the new and enforced collective meme.

Unfortunately, if you are in grade 5 and you still believe in your imaginary friend, you are most likely in a bit of trouble. Your parents and the grownups around you are most likely getting a little worried and might be considering sending you to a psychiatrist. It is quite possible that some of these psychiatrists might even end up prescribing one of the many child drugs that seem to be so popular now, like Ritalin.

Your peers, your classmates in grade 5, have for the most part all been swayed into this new and more powerful belief system or meme. If you go around playing with your imaginary friend, it is most likely that you are getting picked on. Now you are beginning to see the power of what a meme can do to the collective conscious of the people around you. How this belief system can draw them closer and allow them to work in a mob like fashion to push aside any that do not fit within the system. Bullying, ostracizing, and all sorts of other creative abuses might be perpetuated on you at this time if you continue to play with your imaginary friend.

And God help you if you are still playing with your imaginary friend in high school. Here this collective 'mind set' has taken gigantic proportions. Many adults looking back at high school speak of how incredibly hive like the kids in high school can be. For the most part they are quite correct, if you are playing with an imaginary friend during this time or doing anything that does not conform to the highly controlling society of a typical high school, you are in deep trouble indeed. I suppose you could believe in vampires but only if they are of the Twilight[4] variety. Suicides and murders are not unheard of and any that would step outside of the collective mimetic/memetic structure can pay the ultimate price.

---

[4] Interestingly, there are many belief systems or memes that seem to perpetuate a paranormal interest in high school. The thing is though that if you look at these flights of fancy, you will see that they are highly structured and usually take on a rather comical nature. For example, the vampires from the twilight series are highly stylized protagonists that have more to do with propagating ideas/memes on typical teenage angst. Many a teenage girl might wish with all her heart that such a vampire might really exist and take her away from the terrors of her life, but deep down the comical nature of the James Dean looking vampire, that glows in sunshine like a jewel and wants to forever be a high school student, seems too ludicrous to be real even for a still maturing mind.

> *Adults should not be so hasty in their scorn of the typical teenager. Compared to the tightly organized societal structure in which most adults exist; with their complex rituals, governments, religious affiliations, and binding law structures, the average high school environment is not so bad. High school, generally speaking, is just one more step up the ladder into a completely controlled belief structure.*

Looking at it in this way we can see how our years of childhood development into the finality of adulthood is really just a highly focused and incredibly powerful indoctrinating system. One that allows for very little deviation from a structured belief system that is beneficial to most. Beneficial to most because this structured 'matrix' that we have created for ourselves, as the collective human psyche, does indeed provide us with the ability to create highly organized social structures that benefit the many...but there is a cost.

This cost is exacted on the few and on the perceptual capabilities and possibilities of the many:

- While there are fringe elements within any society, those that will not completely adhere to the societal belief structure, these fringe individuals are controlled in a number of ways that makes any kind of revolution or anarchy nearly impossible.

- The cost is also felt among the many, because as a collective homogeny the human race sets huge limits upon itself and its capabilities.

Since we are interested in making fundamental changes, we need to explore the very basics of this indoctrination system and how it affects us as individuals.

> *We need to study this structured belief system so that we may understand how to escape it!*

We know that our beliefs can affect how we perceive and what we consider to be possible within this world. This belief structure might be so powerful that it could actually be changing the way our senses 'can' perceive the world. Since beliefs dictate how we see the world, what we pay attention to, and what we ignore, they are definitely changing our neural structure. Belief systems change our brains.

Since belief systems control what we focus on and what we ignore, they are directly responsible for what part of our brain we engage in what parts we ignore. Generally speaking the nerve structures of our brain increase in number and complexity the more that we use them.

Through functional magnetic resonance imaging (fMRI) scientists are beginning to discover amazing things about how we use our brains. For example, they are beginning to discover that there is indeed a subconscious, one that is capable of engaging certain parts of the brain while completely ignoring conscious awareness. By studying the results of placebos on different subjects they have noted that beliefs play an incredibly important role in how our brains function; that a belief in the certainty of a medication will engage the deep subconscious part of ourselves that can alter the brain's physiology in order to suit those beliefs. In other words, a belief is so strong that it can actually change how your brain functions and by concentrating on this belief over a long period of time you can indeed change the physiology of the brain through nerve conditioning.

In order to make a fundamental change in our cognitive abilities, we do not need to fight the system. There is no need to take up arms or to create some kind of revolutionary cause the will somehow overthrow some giant organization. This organization is created through our own participation and we can begin the process of extricating ourselves from it and expanding our capabilities by taking responsibility for our own beliefs.

Put in another way, there is no need to take on the big belief systems like:

- Religion
- Politics

In order to begin to make a change within yourself, you need to explore more fundamental beliefs like:

- Color: is my red the same as your red? Who said red was red?
- Names: who came up with the original names? Why can't I make up my own names?

Try repeating the word house over and over again until the word becomes silly in your mind. Why don't I think that all words are silly?

- Breathing: do I need to breathe? Is the way that I'm breathing right? Is there a better way to breathe? Am I seeing breathing as something that it might not be? If rocks could, would they think that my breathing is stupid since they don't have to do it? Why don't rocks breathe?

P.S. Science has an answer to all of these questions but who said that it was right? Try to come up with your own answers and remember that since it is impossible for you to verify scientific experimental conclusions, you are essentially taking what they have to say on faith. Perhaps you should start believing in yourself.

These things might seem quite silly but they represent fundamental beliefs that we all have, that quite possibly you have never questioned. Every single thing around you is perceived the way it is because of a belief structure that was imposed upon you from the day of your birth (and if telepathy is real, from a time even before you were out of the womb). If you question those fundamental things that make up your reality, then you begin to systematically restructure that belief system that was taught to you. Just like repeating a word over and over again, this type of fundamental questioning begins to allow a part of you to look at these beliefs in a different way. This slight alteration in how you perceive the reality about you can have some dramatic effects.

Repeating the word 'house' over and over again, might make you think that the word house seems rather silly after a while. Thinking about why red is red and who said that red was red might make you think that red is silly as well and might also make you question the idea of how the rest of the people around you see the world 'out there'. Indoctrination will definitely kick in here; many will consider their questioning to be stupid. But it is these fundamental questions that begin to open up the possibility of a different way of perceiving reality.

Life is what it is because of what we believe. Life maintains its structured order because of our lack of desire or inability to question the beliefs that we have about the reality 'out there'. Begin to question all the simple things you take for granted around you. Question the labels that you use to understand your life. See if you can get that silly feeling about those things round you just like you can when you repeat a word over and over again. Stretch this feeling as much as you can and see if it begins to jolt a part deep inside of you. Don't let fear stop you; the fear that you're wasting your time or the fear that you might end up losing your mind is there because these beliefs are so fundamental to your existence that questioning them implies a form of insanity.

If you wish to go beyond what you believe is possible, this is where you begin.

POINTS TO REMEMBER:

- You are what you believe.

- You perceive what you believe that you can perceive.

- From the minute that you are born the world around you imposes its beliefs upon you. If telepathy is real then this imposition begins before you are even out of the womb.

- Memes are like viruses except that they can now move far quicker and cause much more damage. By understanding the power of memes we can understand how beliefs can control large groups of people.

- Memes are not just responsible for what religion we believe in or what political system we follow, they also explain our perceptions.

- In order to change your perceptions and to get out of the indoctrination forced upon you, you do not need to start a revolution or create a new religious movement. You need to begin by questioning your most fundamental beliefs.

CHAPTER 4
THE DOING OF NOT DOING

Finally, we get to try some of the fun stuff!

I had to make sure that you have a foundation of understanding as to why it is that we human beings perceive the world as we do. You needed to understand that most of our perceptive abilities, and as a result our capabilities, are the result of what we believe and what we have been told to believe since our birth.

This is a very important point and one that you must pursue on your own if it has not become clear to you yet:

> *Beliefs are very important; they control what you will experience in this life. If you wish to expand your psychic abilities, then you need to be able to truly believe that you can change how you see the*

world. That by changing the beliefs that you have, you can begin to realize that the world, and our perceptions, are far more malleable than we might presume. That there is magic just around the corner if we only allow ourselves to believe that we can see it and use it.

I tried to make this as apparent as I could in these early chapters and I have some examples of books that you might wish to read in order to explore this point further in 'recommended reading' at the end of the book. You will not be able to expand your psychic abilities to any great extent until you believe that you are far more capable than you realize, and that the only thing that is holding you back is what you are willing to believe about yourself and the world around you.

Beliefs can be a tricky thing. It can be very difficult to deal with them, especially when they are beliefs that you've had your entire life; beliefs that are continually imposed upon us not only by ourselves but by the collective human psyche.

The old schools knew that this endeavor was a tough one. They knew that the average disciple needed a bit of convincing before they were willing to make the effort required to change their entire psyche. Because of this they came up with some very interesting methods to try and break the great momentum of a lifetime of learnt beliefs.

Instead of trying to change a person's belief, which can be very difficult even with a person's full cooperation, they instead decided to focus their efforts on **breaking routines**.

A routine is a sequence of actions that you regularly follow. The old schools knew that each belief, or grouping of beliefs, creates a conditioned response from an individual. We now know that if something is repeated over and over again, this physical and mental action changes the structure of the body and the brain. The more that you repeat a certain physical or mental action, the more hardwired that you become at making this action.

If for example you are a tennis player, your neural structure and the nerve structures that control the swinging of a racket will become far denser than those structures that are responsible for actions that you don't perform often. These highly used nerve structures will become far more dense and numerous creating a superhighway of nerve connections and complex neural structures. Your muscles, sinew, and bone will also change over time in order to facilitate and further increase your ability to swing a racket and play tennis.

Since our beliefs control our actions, they are also largely responsible for much of our nervous structure. Since it is very difficult to change these highly conditioned and long-standing beliefs, it is far easier to try and break these conditioned neuronal structures by breaking the conditioned response that these structures create. In other words, the way to do this is to break the routines created by a set of beliefs.

Put simply, breaking your perceptual routines allows you to see things that you have not seen before. By breaking a perceptual routine, you break a conditioned reflex which opens the door for you to perceive things in a different way. Breaking your routines is sort of like repeating the word house over and over again; repeating the word house over and over again breaks the routine of only using a certain word a number of times, this break in routine allows you to perceive the word house in a different way.

In this chapter we will explore ways to break these routines.

Breaking perceptual routines in order to facilitate a broader understanding of the reality 'out there' has been used by many old schools throughout history.

- Any kind of ritual behavior is a type of routine break. Rituals usually involve highly stylized actions and procedures that are not to be found in regular life (think of a Christian mass for example). By performing these rituals, a perceptual break is created that allows the awareness of an individual to break from its usual perceptual boundaries and limitations.

- The term weird in the English language actually refers to this kind of routine break. Usually by doing something weird you begin to perceive the Weird around you. Weird begets weird; it breaks perceptual routine and creates perceptive expansion.

A very interesting methodology to break these routines was practiced by the ancient Taoists of China. Their name for these exercises was: Wu-wei

This term is usually now defined as not-doing. Through modern interpretation, thanks to old writing that have survived the centuries, most believe that wu-wei is all about knowing when to act and understanding the natural flow of the world around us.

Wu-wei is actually far more complicated and has to do with the ability of the body and being to act without conscious attention. Beyond this, wu-wei represents a highly complex and very powerful 'routine break' created by ancient Taoists to try and break the perceptual barriers imposed on its disciples. Taoists believed, like all other ancient schools following these traditions, that if wu-wei was practiced long enough, a huge perceptual break would occur. This perceptual break would be so monumental that it would change the entire life of the disciple and would take him or her into the realm of an enlightened immortal[5].

Any type of routine break or not-doing can be practiced by anyone and if it is practiced long enough it will allow you to have a perceptual break. Don't worry, you will not have a monumental change that will turn you into an immortal, not that this sounds like such a bad thing. Perceptual breaks created using this methodology will usually be experienced through small perceptual oddities that can nevertheless scare the wits out of you. Unless you're a hard-core practitioner, or have a teacher to show you the way and make sure you keep going, your first big scare is more than enough to show you just how malleable our awareness is.

Here I'm going to show you some methods you can try in order to break your perceptual routines and begin to see the world from a different angle. There is no need for you to make a monumental change, these practices can be used to cement the idea within your mind that it is only beliefs and conditioned perceptual routines that control how you see the world around you. If you are completely gung ho

---

[5] Since most of our perceptual reality is really based on imposed belief systems, is it not possible that those that can transcend these imposed limitations can also transcend their death? Who said you had to die? Who said you had to die at 70 and not at 170 or at 1070?

about doing not-doing on a hard-core basis, then please listen to my words:

Go Slow!

Let us learn then about the Weird, about the 'odd practices', about the 'not-doing' that can begin to truly open up your mind to greater possibility. Let us examine 'the way' that will allow you to begin to cut the shackles that hold you to 'the matrix' of life.

Here is a list of 'not doings' that you can try:

- Most of our perceptual awareness involves the act of looking at something. Whenever we wish to perceive something, we look at it. We seldom look at things that we do not wish to see, and everything that we perceive has a boundary. Our world therefore is made up of the empty and the full. There is space and then there is object. We are conditioned to only look at the object and to completely ignore the space. The space might define the object because it helps us to understand the boundaries that we place upon these objects that make up our existence but we seldom consider this space to be consequential. Space is generally seen as the real estate that we try to acquire in order to add more objects.

    A great not-doing therefore is to look at space. Find a quiet place where you can take a comfortable position and for 15 minutes try to look at all the space around you and ignore the objects. If you're in a room for example, try to look at where the furniture is not. Look at the space beneath tables, look at the space above the furniture, and look at every inch of empty space around you. Furthermore, look at this space intentionally, don't just look at it how we usually look at space; which is a non-focused type of way that is more akin to something that we do when are daydreaming and looking without seeing. Intently focus on the space that you see before and you and try to see something there, try to focus on that space.

You can also go for a walk and as you are walking try to notice the space around you instead of the objects. Of course, it pays to be careful and there are certain objects that you should not ignore (like cars and trees for example). As you walk, completely shift the attention that you usually give to the world by placing your attention on that which you never pay attention to.

If you are outside and find a lovely area where you can sit and stare at a nice full tree, try to look at this tree by staring at the spaces in between the leaves. In this case try not to look at the object itself but at the boundary that makes up the object, the space around it and within it that defines its identity. By looking at the spaces in between the leaves you begin to understand space as a boundary that creates a definition of what the object that you are looking at is.

Try to do each of these exercises for a minimum of 15 minutes. Take stock of yourself after performing this exercise, see if you can extend the length of these exercises to at least an hour.

- A variation of the above exercise involves the act of looking at the shadows of objects. Just like spaces, shadows are always overlooked and yet they play a key role in how we define space. On a sunny day or in a well lit room, begin to look at the shadow of an object. Try to look at the shadow of this object for 15 minutes and then extend that to an hour if you can. Over time you might begin to notice that the shadow is sort of like glue that holds an object in place, see if you can get that feeling for yourself. Explore whatever feelings you do have.

- Whenever we do something, we do it for a reason. It is seldom the case that you will do something for no reason at all. Science tells us that we are always trying to get the most done for the least amount of effort in order to save energy, that this is the natural inclination of biological life. Science will even try to explain away the act of playing and having fun by proposing the idea that fun and play are a form of complex learning and social jostling.

A great not-doing is to do something for absolutely no reason at all. Perhaps if you want you can take a bunch of books and stack them like a column in the middle of your room. After you are done this, you could take the column down or put it somewhere else. You could start jumping up and down and waving your arms, not because you want to get exercise but for no reason at all.

Explore this idea and try to do things for no reason, especially if those things take some effort to do. For example, you could completely rearrange the furniture in your house so that it all faces in one direction. You could keep this furniture this way for no reason at all. Explore what you feel when you do this. Explore what you feel when others look at what you have done and think of you as being rather crazy.

- A magnificent way to disrupt your regular routines is to begin to laugh for no reason at all. Laughing for no reason goes completely against any kind of idea that you have about reasonable behavior. At first laughing for no reason takes a bit of effort but if you continue you will eventually find yourself laughing hysterically for no reason at all. Continue laughing like this for as long as you can, you will find that it is actually a very physically tiring act.

- A wonderful not doing to try, is the amnesia game. You can either find a quiet place to sit down or go for a nice long walk and pretend that you have amnesia. Pretend that you can't remember anything that happened to you just a second ago and therefore you have absolutely no idea what's going to happen or who or what you might run into in the future. Pretend that you can't remember anything and the only thing you know for certain is what you are looking at right now. If you begin to think about something that you did in the past or you begin to think about something that you want to do in the future, bring yourself back to the idea of pretending to be suffering from amnesia. Try to do this for 15 minutes at first and then extend it to an hour.

- Here is the ultimate routine breaker, try to do something absolutely crazy in public. Now I do not recommend this to everyone and I do think that you should be most careful where you do this, I shall definitely not take any responsibility for something that happens to you while you do this. But one of the greatest ways to break the perceptual routines of life is to do something completely odd while in the presence of others. You might for example begin to laugh for absolutely no reason or perhaps start doing jumping jacks in a public place. Your mind will go crazy here; all sorts of ideas about who you are and what you should be doing in public will come spilling into your mind. Now if you are considered a bit of a nut to begin with and you tend to do weird things in public all the time, then this not-doing might not be extremely powerful for you but for the average person this type of routine breaker is perhaps the most powerful one there is.

These exercises in routine break have a type of cumulative effect, the more that you do them the more that they have a type of destabilizing effect. The first thing that you might notice is that you begin to look at things from more than just one perspective. This ability to see things in different ways allows you to have a greater perception of what's going on around you but it can also make you a little addle brained at times. The reason for this is that you are considering more than you were a while ago and you are therefore thinking longer which can cause you to make mistakes.

Many report that they start to develop a certain type of energy when they do not-doing exercises for a while. They tend to develop a certain type of inner strength that can be applied to other things in their lives. The reason for this is that these exercises expand what you believe to be possible and therefore always provide a type of choice. Things are this way and they have always been this way but now you realize that they could have been this way as well.

You also begin to realize that the way you perceive things is a type of choice, a type of choice that you are making on a constant basis. Discovering the fact you have this choice and the fact that you are making this choice regularly, develops your willpower. A robot has no need of willpower because it just carries on doing whatever is programmed in its memory banks, but a free being needs to have will in order to go in a certain direction. Because you have a choice you develop will and the small taste that you get of this, thanks to these exercises, allows you to grasp this feeling of power. You can then begin to use this will/feeling on other things.

Not-doing exercises develop your will!

It is also possible that after you do these exercises for a while, for some people not very long at all, that your world might seem like it's falling apart. This can be quite scary and can cause you to completely abandon these routine breaking exercises. It is definitely the scariest thing there is, to begin to see the world in a different light and to fundamentally begin to believe that the world around you is far stranger than you thought. It is akin to seeing a unicorn and being forever robbed of the perceptual innocence that you had before; thinking that the world was black and white and could never hold such mystery.

If this becomes the case, then I suggest that you use that new understanding and your developing willpower to try and realize that just because the world is more than you imagined, it doesn't need to be insane. You can have the Weird alongside with the 'normal'. It is for this reason that I recommend to you that you take these exercises slowly.

> *Once you make a breakthrough in how you perceive the world using these not-doing exercises, you might want to take it easy for a while. Come back to these exercises after a while, when you have cemented these new realizations. Proceed in the slow fashion like this, making incremental gains in your perceptive abilities and then allowing these new realizations to cement themselves within your psyche. In this way you will not feel the complete onslaught that can come to those that explore the boundaries of their perceptions.*

Finally, I recommend that you start a little journal. Keep a log of the exercises that you are doing, all of the ones that I will mention to you in this book. Be systematic about when you are doing these exercises and for how long. Record if you increase the length of these exercises and also record what these exercises are doing to you. Explore your feelings and your subjective reality so that you begin to notice if there is any gradual change in how you perceive yourself and the world around you.

CHAPTER 5
SEEING AURAS / ENERGETIC PERCEPTION

As we have discussed in the first chapter, science believes that we are made of atoms. Since science knows that atoms are really vibrational energy then in essence we are vibrating energy. We are not the objects that we perceive ourselves to be.

We also explored the fact that every single thing around us is made up of this vibrational energy. That in actuality everything that we see around us, even what we considered to be empty space, is actually vibrating energy. We also took a look at the electromagnetic spectrum and discovered that our eyes can only see a very small amount of the energy that makes up all of the things around us.

In this chapter we are going to explore the possibility of perceiving a little more of this electromagnetic spectrum. A slight bit more is nothing compared to the entirety of all that is out there but it is enough to allow us to increase our perceptions of the world. I'm going to teach you how to see auras and how to be able to sense energy with your hands and forearms.

Now if you tell the average person that you can see an aura, they tend to think that you are either a bit of a nut or full of bull. It is incredibly hard for the average person to even conceptualize the fact that there is something more out there that can be perceived right now by anyone, if only they were to change their beliefs and visual focus just a bit. The fact of the matter though is that perceiving auras is not a very difficult thing and once you have learnt how, you will be amazed that you hadn't been able to do this all your life.

If you know anything about eye structure, then you will know that your retina has two different kinds of photoreceptors (these receptors pick up light and they are what make it possible for you to see), these are:

- **Cones** which are active at higher light levels, are capable of color vision, and are largely responsible for spatial acuity.

- **Rods** which are responsible for vision at low light levels and are not capable of perceiving color to a great degree.

We are all pretty good at functioning with our cone receptors and we are quite confident about what we are seeing. Few people though realize that most of their night vision is brought about through the rods and without them you would be essentially blind that night.

In order to see auras, you need to learn how to use your rod photoreceptors better. These rod receptors are actually able to pick up a different range of the electromagnetic spectrum than can the cones; they can see a little more into the ultraviolet and infrared. By training yourself to use the rod receptors, you will be able to pick up *subtler* energy frequencies.

In order to do this, let us begin by doing an exercise which will allow you to literally see how the rods work. I suggest that you wait until night time and then turn off all the lights in a room. Allow your eyes to slowly adjust to the low light levels. It is preferable that there is some light in the room so that you can see a little bit.

When your eyes have adjusted and you can actually see a bit of the room around you, try to focus on an object in the room. That is, try to look at an object in the room and see what happens. You will notice that if you try to look at an object directly it becomes very difficult to make out that object clearly. Next try to look at this object from the corner of your eye. For example, you could look a little above the object that you wish to see or little to the side, but try to keep your attention on that corner vision. You will notice that through this corner vision you are able to perceive the object far more clearly.

The reason for this is that the rods are not spread evenly in your retina; most of them are actually around the periphery of your vision so in order to activate them properly you need to be able to look at things through the corner of your eye. To increase your night vision, try to navigate this dark room by looking at things through the corner of your eyes, in this fashion you will be using your rod receptors. I'm sure that you will be amazed at how much more you can see by using your peripheral vision.

You will also notice that this increased night vision seems to dissipate quickly. What's going on here is that the rods contain a rose pigment that is called 'visual purple' and it is this pigment that allows you to see clearly with your rods at night. This visual purple is easily used up but you can easily regain your visual acuity by slightly altering the rods that you are using to see. To do this what you need to do is look at things through the corner of your eye (or your peripheral vision) and at the same time keep your eyes darting back and forth.

As you navigate the dark room that you are in, look at things through the corner of your eyes and keep your eyes darting back and forth or perhaps in a circle. In this way you will be using different parts of your retina which will allow the visual purple to replenish itself quickly.

Using this nifty trick you should greatly increase your night vision. Beyond this, this experiment gives you a good idea as to how the rod receptors work. The next step is to be able to engage these rods and cones simultaneously so that you are actually able to perceive the energetic radiation that surrounds everything around you.

> *When the average person looks at someone else, the only part that they are aware of visually is the body. Because the cones are used and most people are so used to using these and nothing else in order to see the world around them, they tend to believe that this is the only thing that is possible for anyone to see. As we already know the body is actually vibrating energy and through habitual perceptual routine, we tend to see this body as a solid object. Pretend for a moment then, since it might be most difficult to truly believe this now, that this solid object that you think is the body is actually vibrating energy; you can imagine how this body could be similar to a candle flame. The core of the flame itself is very dense and because of that it has the ability to interact with the other dense matter that surrounds it. Just beyond the body/flame, there is a frequency of energy that is slightly denser than the air around it; this frequency of energy is sort of like the heat that is given off by the flame. It is not dense enough to affect the denser material around it to a great degree and it usually extends about half an inch from the body. This heat like radiance is called the Etheric body by most Western Mystics.*
>
> *The next layer which can be easily seen by someone who knows how to see auras, is sort of*

> *like the light that is given off by the candle flame; it is most often called the emotional body. This radiation is even less dense than the other two and usually extends quite a distance around the body. Those that can see this energy level usually describe it as somewhat egg shaped.*

Pretending, for now, that your being is made up of different frequencies of energy of varying intensity, you can begin to use the above analogy; that we are all like a living flame. Like a candle flame, our inner core is made up of a dense material that nevertheless shimmers and radiates large amounts of energy. While our eyes can perceive the core essence (the body/flame), they are not able to perceive the radiation that this body radiates; at best most people that haven't been taught how to see auras can only perceive this exuded energy with their hands.

You can teach yourself to see this energy instead of just perceiving it through your skin as a slight displacement. Thanks to this special ability, you will be able to understand far more about the subtleties of the flame/body before you.

> *Being able to perceive energy with your skin is simple and can be done by anybody. Take your right hand and slowly brush it over your forearm about 2 inches from the skin; when you do this you will feel a slight displacement on your*

forearm. It is possible that you might also feel some heat that is given off by the body and you might even pick up some small air displacement on the fine hairs of your arm. Concentrate though on this displacement feeling because it is this sensation that you are after. This displacement is caused by all the energy radiated by your body; what you are feeling is essentially your aura.

Believe it or not, your forearms are designed to be incredibly receptive tools. The fine hairs on your forearms can pick up any kind of electric energy around you, they can also pick up slight shifts in wind and air pressure. By concentrating on the incredibly sensitive skin of your forearms and the fine hairs there, you should eventually be able to increase your perceptive abilities within any geographical area. With these incredible receptors you will be able to pick up bioelectrical energy, static energy, shifts in air and wind pressure, and eventually even sense the presence of another living entity.

In order to exercise these amazing receptor organs, practice walking around the rooms in your house while paying as much attention as you can to the feelings in your forearms. Over time you will become far more sensitive to these feelings and with little practice you should be able to start using your forearms and hands to great advantage.

In order to clearly perceive your first aura try the following:

1. Have a friend stand in front of a white, gray or pale colored wall. Dim the light in the room but do not block it out completely, you want a twilight effect.

2. Have your friend stick out his or her thumb approximately 6 inches from their face or body. Try to relax yourself as much as possible and focus on the tip of the thumb; what you want is the thumb to be completely in focus making the person's body then slightly out of focus.

3. While maintaining your focus on the thumb, try to pay attention to the body of your friend that is now blurred. If you are very relaxed and you have the lighting at a good level, you will be able to see a thin corona or a mist of white or blue light around your friend.

4. Try moving your eyes about while still maintaining that blurred focus on your friend's body. If you are having trouble, go back to the thumb and try again. When you are able to maintain that blurred effect, try looking around the head and shoulders of your friend darting your eyes back and forth. You might be able to start picking up colors and these displacements might even turn into flares of energy that seem to radiate from your friend.

5. Have your friend take a deep breath and think about something that they really like. Notice if there is any change in the aura that you are looking at. Notice color changes or intensities.

6. Now have your friend take another deep breath and think about something that they really hate. Again, see if there's any change in the aura.

7. As you are doing all this, try to memorize the feeling of what you're doing. The procedure is not very important in this case because it is quite simple. What is far more important is that you remember this feeling that you get from doing this exercise. Using this memory feeling, you will be able to duplicate this perceptive ability in the future.

Once you have the basic idea of how this works, and you have a good internal feeling memory of what it feels like to do it, you need to go out there and practice seeing auras as much as possible. Any place where there's lowlight will allow you to see auras clearly at first. Eventually you will be able to see auras in most lighting conditions. If you are having troubles then most likely you are having troubles relaxing yourself and allowing yourself to believe that you are seeing what you are seeing. Any Problems that I have ever encountered with people not being able to do this has had to do with their ability to relax and just get over their initial skepticism.

With enough relaxation and practice you will be amazed that you had not been able to see this energy before. My personal opinion is that we have always been able to see this energy but we usually block this perception out because our collective psyche tells us that it doesn't exist.

When it comes to colors, there is great variation between different sources. It is my opinion that you should practice seeing auras as often as you can and that you make up your own catalog and reference guide of colors and what they mean.

Here is a general reference that you might want to work with until you build up your own reference guide:

- **Brown:** inflated ego with a deep desire to win at all cost
- **Beige:** dependent and cowardly
- **Olive, drab:** lying, deceit, and jealousy
- **Green, lime green:** usually indicates high energy and intention
- **Yellow:** tends to usually indicate charisma or mental energy
- **Pink:** is usually loving energy

These are just some basic color references so you can get started. Once you have built up a good reference of colors and what they mean, you will find it very easy to be able to look at people and understand their intention. This is very handy when you need to know if someone is lying or when you want to know what their next move is going to be. The aura can tell you about the flame.

Before I mentioned that you can feel the heat from the candle and realize that there are energy frequencies there that you cannot perceive visually. You can use your hands therefore to perceive the slight bit of heat that a body generates but you can also use your hands to be able to sense the energy around every person and thing.

> *Try this exercise:*
>
> *Put one hand out with an open palm.*
>
> *Use your other hand to caress your firsthand but do not actually touch the other hand. Try to keep your secondhand at least an inch away from your outstretched palm. Make swirling motions with your right hand.*
>
> *Now completely ignore your caressing hand and see if you can sense anything with the other. Close your eyes and notice if you can feel any displacement. Try changing the way that you are swirling your hand and see if that makes any difference.*

If you are like most people, you will instantly feel something on the hand and forearm that is stationary. If you don't then just try and relax more and keep at it, you will eventually be able to pick up either heat or a slight displacement. Practice doing this exercise as often as you can.

If you are lucky, see if you can get a friend to help you; try to sense the energy displacements from their body using the ethereal caress method mentioned above. See if you can feel any displacements along the body, especially around the areas where there are supposedly Chakras[6].

With practice you should find it easier and easier to see the energy around you and eventually to identify large energy vortexes. With practice you should also have a greater ability to be able to discover the intentions of the people around you, either identifying their intentions through the color of their auras or perhaps even a slight shift in the kind of energy that you feel is exuding from them.

---

[6] A Chakra is a whirling vortex of energy. Since different belief systems have different numbers of Chakras and sometimes these tend to be in different positions throughout the body, it is a good idea for you to try and figure out where these vortexes are on your own and see if they match up to anything in literature. Any place where there's a large concentration of nerve fibers, like the solar plexus, is most likely going to hold a huge amount of energy and will indeed be a Chakra.

If you get a chance to go outside or to find yourself in what would be called a paranormal area, try to use the technique of looking at things through the corner of your eyes. Using this technique you might be able to pick up on color alterations in your field of vision which will denote some kind of energy vortex. In this way you can scan the ground or different objects in order to see if they have some kind of abnormal energy to them. This energy does not necessarily have to be paranormal, but any large source of electromagnetic energy should create a small displacement and these electromagnetic sources usually feed supernatural phenomenon in the area. Areas with highly concentrated electromagnetic fields will usually exhibit paranormal phenomena.

You can also use your enhanced vision to look for ghosts which can sometimes have enough energy to them to be able to create a small auric field which you should be able to see with enough practice. This is all about practice, anyone who is relaxed and confident enough can get good at this technique. Also remember to use your kinesthetic sense, feel around the area. Once you practice the methods mentioned above, you should also be able to pick up small energy displacements with your forearms and hands.

Take the challenge and go out there and discover the world that had been invisible to you just a little while ago. Expand your capabilities with practice and the desire to see. You will eventually discover the amazing complexity of the world around you. If you can master the methods outlined in this chapter, you can begin to use your body and its enhanced senses to point you in the direction of all the paranormal activity around you.

CHAPTER 6
BREAKING THE BIGGEST ROUTINE OF ALL

We have explored the idea that what we see 'out there' is the result of beliefs. Hopefully you are becoming aware of the incredible power of beliefs over your perceptive abilities, and you have begun to explore on your own what kind of beliefs you hold. I also recommend that you try and read some of the books I've mentioned, that you at least begin to explore on your own different sources that are compatible with your interests and desires.

Whatever those interests might be, remember that it is your beliefs that set limits so try and step outside of those rigid beliefs that you had in the past and perhaps explore new belief systems that might allow you to go beyond your hitherto limitations.

As we have discussed these beliefs that we hold are so strong that they can actually change our brains. These beliefs create certain neural pattern in our brains which are enforced and reinforced during the course of our lives through repetition. Our beliefs therefore create a repetitive pattern that reinforces itself even on a biological basis. This repetitive pattern is a routine that we take for granted and use as a type of salve to make us feel better, to make us feel happy and complacent in the world that we think we understand completely.

Our routines make us feel warm and cozy and while feeling this way is not a bad thing, hypnotizing ourselves into believing that this is the only way of things, can be quite dangerous.

One of the greatest routines that we have, perhaps even the greatest, is our sleep cycle. We tend to go to sleep at a certain time and to get up at the time that we feel is appropriate. This repetitive pattern has very little to do with natural human sleeping cycles and is actually completely controlled by what we believe.

> *It is now believed by scientists that our circadian rhythm (our biological clock) is greatly controlled by the Sun. That is, if people were left to their own devices, people would sleep all night and wake up during the day naturally. It is the case though that more natural people, hunter-gatherers living far away from civilized areas, tend to have a sleep cycle that is highly varied. They do not sleep all night and wake up all day*

> *but quite often sleep in short segments during the day and night.*
>
> *Anyone who's spent a long time in nature and away from the civilized world begins to realize that their sleep cycles tend to take on a highly varied nature. To believe that we are supposed to be only awake during the day and that somehow we are fearful and highly ill-disposed creatures at night is silly. More natural people throughout the world demonstrate that human beings are quite capable of maneuvering and existing at night with great success, they demonstrate that they do not need to have a halogen lamp attached to their foreheads to go to the washroom and to hunt.*

Our beliefs tell us that we need eight hours straight of sleep or more. They tell us that if we do not have this kind of sleep we will start to deteriorate and that our functioning will be impaired.

We follow our routines without question, waking up when the buzzer sounds and groggily get ready to go to work. At night we make sure that we go to sleep every evening at a certain time to make sure that we get those eight or more hours, chastising ourselves if we break this pattern. We tend to feel that something is wrong with us if for some reason we can't sleep at night and instantly look for some kind of remedy, all the while worrying about how much our next they will be compromised by our lack of sleep this night.

This sleep cycle of course is highly dubious. Something that can be easily proven by looking at human sleep cycles through even the short amount of history that we have recorded and have access to:

- Our earliest ancestors, that we know of, were the hunter-gatherers; there sleep cycle, which can be correlated with the hunter-gatherer societies that still exist in the world, were highly varied. They tended to do many things at night and would also take long sleep breaks during the day. Contrary to popular opinion, there are not as many human predators at night as there is during the day which makes the night a wonderful time to go hunting for certain prey. Hunter gatherer societies did not sleep for eight hours straight;

They did not sleep all night and stay awake all day!

- The big change came when we began to establish agricultural societies; here is where we get the kind of sleep cycle that we have now. It was during the agricultural era, and is now common with anyone who lives a farmer's life, to sleep all night and then wake up during the day to be able to work in the field. But even during this time, the sleep cycle was not a constant eight hour one; it actually consisted of two chunks. Essentially our very recent ancestors, perhaps even your grandmother and grandfather if they lived in an agricultural setting, would go to sleep early from a hard day of work and then wake up in a few hours. They would stay awake for around two hours and finally go back to sleep again until the next morning. It was during these two hours that much of the fairytale world of our forefathers became alive[7].

- In the modern world; we say that there isn't much difference between night and day. Thanks to our electrical systems we have light wherever we need it. New York for example is the city that never sleeps and there are indeed individuals that live completely nocturnal lives.

Unfortunately, our modern age has not given us greater freedom but a more rigid sense of what sleep is supposed to be. Even those that have completely nocturnal existences, believe that they must have a straight chunk of eight hours or more of sleep. Those that have a 9 to 5 work schedule seem to be almost forced to maintain this kind of sleep cycle. Even though we have far greater capability thanks to our technological advances, we are nevertheless stuck in our beliefs that our sleep cycle needs to be one large chunk followed by a wakeful state that is hopefully as long as possible.

---

[7] If you wish to research this further then you might try looking up the work done by psychiatrist Thomas Wehr. I also recommend the book by Roger Ekirch, "At Day's Close".

The reality of the situation is that our bodies are made to take shorter breaks. Going without food or water for eight hours or more when we are sleeping is not a natural thing, it hurts the body. It is also the case that our wakeful attention needs rest, and after six hours or more of wakefulness the body screams for a break so that it might wake up renewed and more focused. Ever wonder why coffee shops seem to have become so popular?

> *Interesting side notes in Europe are the Spanish. They still hold the belief and therefore practice the routine of taking a large nap during the hottest part of the day. As a result, the Spanish nightlife is legendary and it is the case that the real fun in Madrid is going on in between 11 PM and 7 AM.*

The greatest routine that you can break therefore is the sleep cycle. Breaking this modern sleep cycle is probably one of the greatest things that you can do to begin to experience a wholly different reality. Breaking this sleep cycle is not only sensory enhancing; it is also good for the body.

Breaking the sleep cycle routine will allow you to experience consciously a far greater range of the subconscious, which will incredibly alter the reality that you perceive. Right now we exist in a world that is either highly conscious or completely asleep; I would say 'dead asleep'. As a result, we have separated our lives into the light and the darkness. Even though we have light enough to light anywhere we wish to go, we still fear that which lurks in the angles beyond.

Breaking up the sleep cycle naturally opens up this segregation of the conscious and subconscious mind. Essentially by breaking up your sleep cycle you start to become far more conscious during the times when you previously thought you were dead to the world. You will also begin to experience many interesting perceptual occurrences during your awake time[8]. Your conscious will begin to become more aware of your subconscious and your subconscious will take on a more participatory role during your fully conscious phase.

Being asleep for shorter cycles blurs the division somewhat between sleeping consciousness and wakeful consciousness. You begin to become far more aware of the dreams that you have and the kind of life that you experience while your body sleeps. During wakefulness you are not so consumed by the stark concreteness of the objective world around you. You might say that by changing your sleep cycle your wakeful time becomes less painful and far more fluid.

The sleep cycle that I have had the most success with is one chunk of sleep of five hours followed by a nap

---

[8] These odd perceptual occurrences can be anything from; increased intuition such as flashes of insight or a greater feeling /sense, greater feelings of euphoria, generally a more relaxed state, more creativity, more potent visualizations.

during the day. This nap can be as long as you want but try not to exceed a half hour. You can also vary this by using a large sleep chunk of four hours and then taking two small naps. Ideally any nap that you take should be no more than half an hour.

See if you can dedicate a whole month to changing your sleep cycle following one of the examples I've mentioned above. It will take a bit of time for the good effects of this new sleep cycle to set in, which is why I recommend that you try and do it for a month. In the journal that I've mentioned that you should get, keep a running log of the changes that you experience from your new sleep cycle. At first it will be hard because breaking any pattern is quite hard, but eventually it will become much easier and with this new pattern you will begin to see some amazing changes in your consciousness.

If you have a full-time job, think about staying up later at night making sure that you get your five hours of sleep at night, and then make it a habit of taking a nap right after you get home from work. Let your body adjusts to this rhythm, at first it will seem like you are groggy all the time but this feeling goes away, plus there is some benefit to this grogginess[9].

---

[9] For those that get groggy, try to use this feeling favorably. That grogginess that you feel is actually a very wonderful relaxant that your body produces. Instead of trying to fight it, let it envelop you and use it as a natural relaxant throughout the day; you could say that you are making your own happy feelings without the need for any drugs at all. This natural relaxant also

If you're one of those people that find it hard to get started on this, I recommend that you try doing some hypnagogic or hypnopompic exercises:

- **Hypnagogic** refers to that drowsy half asleep period you experience just before you go to sleep. If you have ever been bored to death while listening to a very boring lecture then you have definitely experienced hypnagogic events.

- **Hypnopompic** refers to that drowsy half-awake state that you experience as you are waking up in the morning from a long night's rest. It's that wonderful time just before you are fully awake when you can just soar between sleeping and waking.

By practicing either hypnagogic or hypnopompic exercises, you will be able to extend the reach of your conscious mind into the sleeping world. Without breaking your sleep cycle, you can practice this form of exercise to go deeper and deeper into your subconscious and dreaming self. These exercises can greatly alter your perception and your physiology, some of these symptoms are:

- If you are practicing hypnagogic exercises, you will initially begin to see mental hallucinations that will usually involve lights and swirling geometric patterns. If you are

---

allows you to quiet your mind and can be an incredible help to those that suffer from nervous conditions of any kind.

practicing hypnopompic exercises then you will most likely go straight into a dream event, unless you have been awake for a while, in which case you might begin by hallucinating swirling lights and geometric patterns as well.

- Sleep paralysis will start to set in. This usually means that your body is basically passing out; the onset of sleep paralysis is what is responsible for all the head bobbing that goes on when someone is just about to fall asleep. Eventually full-body paralysis sets in.

- Just before or just after sleep paralysis, you will begin to experience full on hallucination. This can either take the form of odd mental events such as seeing objects flash before your mind, feeling weird sensations throughout your body, or fully engaged events where you could essentially be said to be dreaming.

- It is also possible that you can begin to experience sound hallucinations during this time. Many report hearing other people talk or perhaps listening to weird buzzing noises.

With either of these exercises, the trick is to wake up just before you go into full sleep. By waking up just before full on sleep, you are able to consciously remember the physiological hallucinations that you have just experienced. With practice you can extend the amount of time that you spend in this 'threshold of consciousness' which can allow you to begin to experience a weird ethereal world where the nature of reality collapses.

In order to perform hypnagogic exercises you can either take a sitting or a lying down position. These exercises are easier to do in a sitting position because:

- Your body seems to have a different conscious state while sitting; hypnagogic effects seem to be more interesting and vivid while in a sitting position.

- It is far easier to keep from falling into a deep sleep since sitting is naturally not a position that most of us use to sleep in the first place.

You can either just find a nice comfortable sitting position and let yourself drift off, using the bob of your head wake you up or you can use an old trick; which involves holding something in your hand that is relatively heavy, when sleep paralysis sets in and your hand loses its grip of the object, you are naturally brought back to consciousness thanks to the clattering sound of the falling object.

In order to do hypnopompic exercises, all you really need to have is a good alarm clock. Instead of waking up just before you have to go to work in the morning, try setting your alarm clock a half hour before you need to wake. When the buzzer goes off in the morning, hit the snooze button and give yourself an extra five or 10 minutes of sleep. When the buzzer rings again, hit the snooze button again and do this for the half-hour extra time that you have. In this way you are essentially allowing yourself to go back to sleep and with the help of the buzzer you will be able to wake up every 10 minutes and, in this way, remember what happened while you in the sleep state. See if you can extend this hypnopompic exercise for an hour, which means you will just have to set your alarm clock an hour before you wake every morning.

Points that can help:

- If you don't seem to be experiencing too much consciously doing these hypnopompic exercises, it could be possible that you need to wake up a little more after your alarm clock goes off the first time. Try sitting up in bed, stretching out, and perhaps doing a few deep inhalations before you try to go back to sleep again. It is sometimes the case that you need to become a little more conscious before you can experience true hypnopompic hallucinations.

- If you have a partner, it might be a good idea to see if you can invest in a hearing-impaired alarm clock. These clocks work just like a regular alarm clocks except that they usually have a pad that goes under your pillow. Instead of an alarm going off, what ends up happening is that this pad under the pillow begins to vibrate; no noise just vibration. In this way you can practice your hypnopompic exercises without waking the person next to you every 10 minutes for an hour.

- Keep a log of all of the hallucinations that you have during these exercises in your journal.

- Try asking yourself questions just before you engage in these exercises and see if the hallucinations that you experience help to answer those questions.

- Try and control the kind of hallucinations that you have and see what kind of will power it takes to be able to change the hallucinations that your experience.

- Try to have an out of body experience while you are performing these exercises.

- Try to live out a fantasy while in the midst of these hallucinations.

- Keep track of the time during these hallucinations; is there a difference between the time that you think you spent in this exercise and the actual time that this exercise took in the objective world? Does time become elastic during these hallucinations? How does this elastic time make you feel?

While the hypnagogic and hypnopompic exercises can truly open your consciousness to greater perceptions, I am hoping that they convince you to eventually change your sleep cycle. The reason for this is that while these exercises can allow you to experience some amazing things while you're doing them, the change in the sleep cycles can completely alter your reality on a full-time basis.

You might say that magic(k) begins to come back into your life when you change your sleeping cycles; perceptions that are usually referred to as hallucinatory phenomena, start becoming far more prevalent in your life. These perceptions are not hallucinations of course but are actually symbolic representations of what is going on inside your subconscious mind. Some of these perceptions are also quite legitimate extrasensory perceptions that become available to you as you begin to blur the lines between the conscious and the sleeping self; between the conscious and the subconscious self.

It is very important that you begin to pay far more attention to the thoughts that you have throughout your day now. All these thoughts have meaning in that they are related to what you are experiencing and feeling. They are your connection to a deeper part of yourself and what they are trying to tell you is very important. By changing your sleep cycle this 'running consciousness' that you usually try to control becomes far stronger. Instead of trying to make it go away with cappuccinos, try to pay attention to it and make it your task to become aware of it throughout your day. As you do so you will realize that much of this running consciousness is actually a symbolic and sometimes quite literal representation of the world around you, moreover it is a greater perception of the world around you. You will discover far more with it then you ever could using your physical senses alone. Your inner and outer mind are meant to work together and when they do, they provide an incredibly rich source of extra-sensory perception.

CHAPTER 7
THE POWER OF BELIEFS

There are more things in heaven and earth Horatio than are dreamt of by your philosophy.
SHAKESPEARE

We have now explored 4 ways in which to see far more than we could have before. Using the:

- not doing exercises
- auric vision
- disrupting sleeping cycles
- hypnagogic and hypnopompic exercises

You should be able to greatly expand your ability to see those things considered paranormal.

These are very powerful techniques and with them alone you should be able to begin an entirely new existence where what is considered the paranormal or the occult is commonplace. With these techniques, and practice, I have fulfilled most of my goal to show you a way to expand your perceptive abilities.

There is one final thing that we must explore though before I can feel confident in saying that I have explained to you all that you need in order to become capable of greater vision and perception. This final thing takes us back to the very beginning of the book; it takes us back to **beliefs**.

The techniques and exercises that I mentioned above did not really require you to change your belief system to a great degree. You needed to just be able to have enough desire to try the different techniques mentioned and then to persist at them until you get positive results.

My hope is that you attempt and continue working with these exercises. If you do, you will be incredibly amazed at the results that you get. As I said, by themselves these exercises will give you the ability to see that which was not perceivable before. They will allow you to experience a greater reality where magic(k) is real and where your consciousness can actually begin to perceive the greater reality around you. Methodically following the regimen of these exercises, you will be able to act with far greater precision and range because of the fact that you have more information available to you.

Essentially you will learn to step in to a new dimensional level, one where you are able to perceive things from different angles; angles that give you more detail and greater depth.

But there is also another aspect to doing these exercises; I am hoping that with time when you get positive results with them, you will be ready to take the final step. This final step is beginning to admit to yourself wholeheartedly that what most consider the supernatural is actually real. By increasing the range of your perception, you will begin to prove to yourself that these paranormal realities do in fact exist.

Once you can truly cement this belief within yourself, you will be able to naturally expand your awareness. While the exercises mentioned above will continue to help you in many ways, in this final phase you will begin a more natural procedure where personal expansion flows seemingly effortlessly. The above exercises though will help in giving you a modicum of control over this expanding awareness so that you are able to channel it and focus your range of perceptions in the direction that you choose.

It is possible for you take a more active role in this fundamental change in beliefs

In order to do this we will practice another exercise that should help you to manipulate your beliefs to a great degree. This exercise can be used on any belief that you have; if you follow the writings on my website, then you will realize that changing beliefs can be very beneficial in all aspects of your life.

Like many things, the exercise is a simple one to describe but it does take strong focus and effort to do it correctly:

- Find a nice quiet environment where you know you will be alone and undisturbed.

- For five to twenty minutes, believe *with every single fiber of your being* that you can see; ghosts, UFOs, aliens, monsters, auric fields, the weird, etc.

- The thing here is to choose something from the above list and focus on it. For example, you might want to believe with every fiber of your being that you can see ghosts, that you have the capability to see these entities and if there is one around you, you can see it now.

- After you are done with the exercise, forget about it and go about your daily business as usual.

- Do this exercise for five days in a row, once a day if you can. After which you might want to take a couple of weeks off and then do it again for five days in a row in a type of repetitive cycle.

As I said this exercise seems easy but it is actually far harder than it first appears. It can be quite a taxing thing to try and believe something with every fiber of your being. It's sort of like playing a game of pretend but one that has to be maintained for a period of time without any relaxation. This can take an incredible amount of concentration and effort and it is quite possible that you might actually begin to sweat from this effort.

Remember your journal and write down when you performed the exercise and any experiences that you might have from doing the exercise. There will be slight changes within you over time and you must record these changes as well so that you keep a log of what is happening to your subjective/mental scape.

What this exercise will do is that it will actually begin to work on your psyche and change old beliefs into new ones. These changes will most likely manifest in odd synchronicities, desires, or perhaps impulses to try things that you might not have wanted to try before. They might give you an odd sense of confidence where you did not have this kind of confidence before. You must record all these subjective and objective perceptions so that you maintain a good reference as to how your psyche is changing over time. This can be invaluable if you wish to replicate a particularly successful experiment.

For example, you might have practiced the above exercise with the intention of seeing ghosts; you might get an odd confidence that can get you out the door and into paranormal areas. It might also provide greater impetus to try the auric exercises for example that could help greatly in this area. It will also begin to change the very structure of your perception so that as you become more disposed to the possibility of seeing ghosts, you begin to activate certain unused perceptive abilities that are latent within you. It is often the case that people begin to notice things that they had completely overlooked in the past, such as air displacements or odd shadows in the corner of their vision.

Once you have done this exercise for a while, I want you to do this exercise again but this time in an area where you know or suspect that there is paranormal activity. If you do not have access to place around you that you know has paranormal activity, try to find a place that *might* have paranormal activity. If even this is hard to find where you live, try to go to a desolate place such as a heavily wooded area.

Doing this exercise in such an environment can be a bit challenging. It becomes challenging because once you start to believe that you can, the reality of the existence of the paranormal becomes very 'real'. Fear will always be the first challenge in seeking the paranormal and it is this fear that you must combat.

By doing this exercise in a spooky area, you begin to naturally combat this desire to flee from that which you actually wish to perceive. You see most paranormal activity is overlooked by the average person because of the fact that they have a deep fear of actually seeing something. There is a lot out there that is strange and different, but most people will naturally turn away from the strangeness because this strangeness causes fear within them. Many people have natural talents and they don't even realize that they have these talents because of the fact that they repress them so that they do not have to experience this fear.

Getting over the fear of the paranormal then is the first step to seeing it. This goes for even the intrepid Ghost Hunter that you see on television. Most of these folks cannot see what they should be able to easily perceive because they are so darn scared of actually seeing that which they supposedly wish to see. For example, most 'out of body' experiences tend to be cut short or are completely forgotten by the individual because such strange events can be so jarring to the psyche that forgetfulness seems prudent.

There will always be an element of fear but you must be able to control this fear at least to an extent. You must fight this fear with curiosity and with a great desire to see and experience more of the world around you. The 5 to 20 minute exercise above will help you to deal first and foremost with this fear.

Once you begin to conquer this fear, you will also begin to expand your perceptive abilities. The world will begin to open up before you as it has never done before and you will take baby steps, perhaps you will crawl, into the land of 'Weird'.

Try to practice the 'belief changing exercise' in as many strange places as you can. It can be quite strange for example to practice this exercise in your backyard looking up at the stars, believing with every fiber of your being that a UFO will appear before you, or that you will have a very personal contact with an entity from a different dimension. The more that you push yourself out of your comfort zone the better.

As I said, this exercise is easy to write about and describe but it is one that will take some effort on your part. Some of this effort is due to the amount of forceful attention that you must use in order to get yourself to believe something for what will seem like a very long period of time. Some of this effort will also come from the fact that this is a highly subjective exercise and as your psyche changes then so must this exercise change ever so slightly for you over time.

What I mean by this is that if for example you practice doing this exercise in order to see ghosts, you will begin perhaps with the general notion of just believing that you can see ghosts. As you do this exercise for a while, you might realize that your fear is really a great block that you must work on. So, you might wish to change this exercise ever so slightly from just seeing ghosts to not being afraid of seeing ghosts.

You see there is a great subjective difference there; in the first instance you just wanted to be able to believe that you see ghosts but in the second instance you are doing the exercise in order to stop yourself from fearing seeing ghosts. Perhaps after you conquer you fear to some extent, you might once again begin to focus on believing that you can now see ghosts all around you. It changes as you change and you have your own highly personal and subjective experiences as you continue with the exercise. It is a fluid methodology that allows you to naturally focus on different aspects of your psyche.

Also, as your perceptive abilities expand, you must continue to use this exercise to expand in all areas. For example, once you begin to see certain ghosts you might wish to use this exercise to help you expand your auric perceptions. Indeed, doing the auric exercises and this exercise together will greatly increase the power of your auric perceptions. This exercise can also be used with any of the other exercise I have shown you so that in a way it is sort of like a strengthening exercise to help you to expand the capabilities of all the others. This exercise feeds on those exercises and those exercises combined with this one will empower your perceptive abilities to an incredible degree!

CHAPTER 8
A ROAD SIGN TO HIGH STRANGENESS

Chapel perilous is an occult term and one that might become all too real for you if you practice the things mentioned in this book.

In the last chapter I mentioned the fact that beliefs can be altered and when these beliefs are altered we experience the first obstacle in the paranormal; this obstacle is fear.

Chapel perilous is a good name for this obstacle. As was traditionally used by Robert Anton Wilson[10], it refers to a state where it is difficult to figure out

---

[10] I recommend any of his books. They are all amazing but if you want to get a direct reference to Chapel perilous and to some of the work that you are doing, if you're following the exercises and the meme of this book, then I suggest the "Cosmic Trigger" trilogy.

whether what you are experiencing is purely imagination or if there is truly something out there.

- The first part/definition of this obstacle has to do with the fearful realization that beliefs are indeed quite plastic and that what you might be witnessing at the moment might only be a personal delusion brought about through a change in belief.

- The other aspect/definition of this has to do with your struggle to determine whether or not there are outside forces, which you are now perceiving, or is it all just a lie (crazy belief) in your mind.

Do you actually believe there is something out there to affect you or is it all just perceptual change through belief? Here is the place where Reasonable Logic dies.

Thanks to the belief changing exercise in the last chapter and with the help of the other exercises that have come before, you will begin to see new things. You will be able to experience a world that you might not have believed existed before. Beyond this you might begin to experience truly strange phenomena such as talking to departed people or having interactions with entities that you might have thought before were part of the fantasy realm.

In his wonderful book, "The Mothman Prophecies" author John Keel[11] begins to explore the subjective state. A state where truly strange and paranormal phenomenon seem to materialize because of the fact that you believe they should. He begins to contemplate seriously the idea that we usually only see in fiction:

> *Which is the idea that once you see the paranormal (or some other paranormal creature); there is no going back to sanity. Now you have become paranormal entity public enemy number one and it will therefore do anything to take you out or drive you mad just to protect its secret existence.*

Keel's conclusions are the same as mine, the Weird exists and is as tangible as this world but there is usually a cloud over it which keeps it hidden from us. Once we see beyond this cloud everything breaks out of Pandora's Box and we can never go back to the sanity that we knew before. What happens to him can be a revelation to those that would explore the hidden angles. Confronted by the truly Weird, you will begin to question your sanity; this questioning is Chapel perilous.

Chapel perilous can be a dangerous place. It is indeed perilous ground and must be tread lightly. There will

---

[11] Please read the book here ("The Mothman Prophecies"), the movie has actually very little to do with the book that was written by John Keel.

come a time when you won't know whether what you are seeing is real or in your imagination.

Indeed, since we have already described in some detail the fact that beliefs are so powerful at creating our reality, the next logical question becomes;

> *Aren't I seeing what I'm seeing only because I believe it?*

Believe it or not (pun?) this is the easy part of Chapel perilous. It is of course not easy at all because it opens up a whole new reality, a reality where anything is possible as long as we are willing to believe completely. The connotations of this possibility are enough to drive some mad; indeed it has driven some into the loony bin.

But the real scary part, the one that can totally end your quest into the paranormal and perhaps put you in a lead lined bomb shelter with tinfoil on your head, is;

> *Are there forces out there right now manipulating me?*

Sorry but I'm not going to tell you that there aren't forces out there manipulating you. This is something that you will have to discover for yourself. What I will tell you though is that there will be a point when you will question your sanity and this questioning can end your career as a paranormal researcher, or aspiring sorcerer if you will.

While Robert Anton Wilson might wish you to become an agnostic, I would rather that you make up your own mind. Certainly, an agnostic would seem to be the better deal in that you don't have to go into a padded cell but the agnostic answer can be the beginning of the end.

An agnostic after all is a person that believes that nothing is known or can be known of the greater existence of nature and God, or the supernatural realm. While this route seems sane, it has always seemed to me that this is a choice made by those that do not have the 'testicular fortitude' to look for the real answers 'out there'. If you are going to go this route, then I suggest that you go at least the way of the Chaos magicians and believe that a belief is just a means to an end[12].

Unfortunately, even the Chaotic route tends to bring an end to most true paranormal study. The reason for this is that believing that beliefs can be switched so easily might afford some form of flexibility (and security) but it does not allow the body to pursue its greater evolution. Most Chaos magicians that I have

---

[12] Chaos magicians follow in old dictum that says that, "nothing is true and everything is permitted". This is a phrase that was supposedly coined by the master assassin, Hassan-i-Sabbah. It basically means that Chaos magicians believe a certain thing until they are able to attain a certain result and then change this belief to something else in order to attain a different result. If you wish to study this magick tradition in greater detail then I suggest any of the books by Phil Hine or Peter Carroll.

met are jaded individuals that tend to really be atheists in disguise.

Indeed, the path that would have you become a paranoid schizophrenic is not a savory one, and I would definitely not want you to end up with a jacket that straps in the back. But in order to truly begin to expand your capabilities, and not become jaded by classifying most of the paranormal as just a different compartment of your mind, you must be willing to go far beyond yourself.

Why? The reason is that belief systems and those changes in perception that you WILL experience by following the exercises in this book are only the tip of the iceberg. There is a greater reality out there and a greater possibility for us all as human beings. Chaos magicians and agnostics are barely touching the tip of this colossal iceberg. They stick their hands into the 'dark sea of perception'[13] and call themselves magicians, a.k.a. Masters of the universe, for what they did. While a child can be satisfied with such small beginnings, there is a point where you must truly take the plunge in order to explore the greater depths.

---

[13] This is a slight modification of a term that is used by Don Juan in the books written by Carlos Castaneda. The actual term is *the dark sea of awareness* and it signifies the chaotic (think math) stew that surrounds us, and the possibilities of our perceptions within it; a perception that has limits but still has the capability of exploring many dark and dangerous places within this infinite sea.

I believe that there are some readers out there that are willing to explore these depths. These depths require a strong character, and some serious cajones!

The reasons for this chapter are twofold:

- The first is to tell you about Chapel perilous and to give you some ideas on how to deal with it.

- The second is to give a basic guide to those that wish to go a little deeper into the great sea of perception.

Hopefully you have a good idea of what Chapel perilous is. There are those that begin to experience this chapel perilous when they see a light or a shadow out of the corner of their eye while there are those that require the entire world to crumble around them before they get any hint of this dark chapel.

Whatever the case might be, remember that this is your first test. It starts out small at first with those pangs of fear that grip you when you experience the unknown but then these pangs grow and grow until you begin to question the very sanity of your mind.

Know then that this test stands before you and be prepared.

So, what do adventurers of the psyche do when they cannot become agnostics? What you do is you look at the great face of Chaos with a strong spirit and a little bit of stink in your eye. You see, there is no way to get around Chapel Perilous, if you doubt me then try to look up an agnostic or a Chaos magician if you can find one. You will not find a great adventurer there, you will just find another man lost in a different routine, perhaps a man who has made a cage for himself that is slightly bigger and perhaps just a little more flexible but it is a cage and therefore a perceptual routine nonetheless.

To go further, what you must do is let Chapel perilous become a dear friend in your life. A constant companion that will always be there filling your life with fear and perhaps even dread. A friend because if you're doing your work right, you will always be able to count on its company.

In the next chapter we will talk about ways to be able survive the great dangers 'out there', in this chapter though let us conclude by examining some of the character traits that you will either develop on your own or work towards attaining in order to be able to withstand the chaos of the great sea of perception.

Just like any explorer embarking on any great adventure, there are certain character traits that you require in order to survive the journey:

- **A great explorer needs to have great discipline**. This discipline cannot be a type of imposed rigidity on the self; it has to be a type of armor placed upon the self in order to satisfy a greater curiosity. Normal human discipline fails in the face of the great onslaught out there, what you need instead of this human discipline is a discipline born of the great desire for exploration; "I am willing to do or to put up with all of this because I will do anything to find out what is out there." Great desire maintains this discipline, not will power.

- **A great adventurer needs to see everything as a challenge.** Every problem faced on the journey must be seen as an obstacle to be overcome, as a challenge to be vanquished through greater discipline and strong imagination. The moment that you see a problem through the eyes of pessimism, you are done.

- **An adventurer on this quest must challenge every single belief that he or she has.** If you don't already, you will soon begin to realize the great power of the beliefs that you hold. With this knowledge it then becomes your responsibility to question these beliefs because they are what shape your reality.

- **As an adventurer you must also question everything that you perceive.** As you take responsibility for your beliefs, you will also take responsibility for what you perceive. But there might come a time, I'm not saying that there will, but there might come a time when what you perceive out there seems even beyond what you believe. When this is the case, examine this perception. This might be the time that you will be faced with a foreign energy source, one that is perhaps beyond yourself.

- **An adventurer requires an incredible amount of temperance.** The only way to truly develop this temperance is through the development of logic. As I have told you before, I do make a distinction between regular logic and reasoning and you should definitely make such distinctions yourself if you plan to explore the great chaos out there. Remember that logic can support any kind of mental structure as long as it's willing to make a reasonable assumption. There is nothing wrong with creating these reasonable assumptions as long as you logically understand that there is every possibility in the world that you can create a completely different mental structure using the same logic and a different reasonable assumption[14].

- **An adventurer needs to trust his/her impulses and his/her feelings.** Do not let the

---

[14] What is the difference between this and chaos magick? The chaos magician is a highly sane individual that pretends that every once in a while he can go insane in order to achieve his desire. A true adventurer on the other hand is an insane (someone who no longer constrains his or her perceptions) individual who creates and catalogs an infinite variety of mental structures (beliefs) and uses them like markers in order to navigate through deep and treacherous waters.

world around you tell you that your impulses, feelings, and desires are wrong or should be ignored. Learn to listen to all of these feelings and study them so that you discover their source. Out there you only have your feelings to guide you so make sure that you start giving them the respect that they deserve.

- **Finally, an adventurer of the great sea of perception needs to take responsibility of his/her consciousness.** You can no longer sit back and allow yourself to be who you are without taking responsibility. You are who you are because of what you perceive and since what you perceive is greatly, or perhaps totally, shaped by your beliefs, you need to take responsibility for this consciousness of yours from now on.

This is a basic outline of the way of the explorer, the way of the true magician or sorcerer. Lacking words to truly name this voyage into the great depths of perception, I hope that you will be satisfied with at least the beginnings of a code. This code has nothing to do with ethics; it is a code that will hopefully allow you to maintain 'yourself' when you are facing the onslaught of the chaos out there.

Above all things remember that discipline as you know it does not work out there, you must develop your own way. While the Buddhists would tell you to lose yourself, I would tell you to build walls around the self and guard it with your life because if you lose it out there, you are truly lost.

CHAPTER 9
THE PROPER USE OF BANISHMENT

Depending on your previous experience, the term **Banishing** can have different connotations for you. Generally speaking banishing is defined as; to send away from, to forbid, get rid of or abolish.

From an occult point of view, banishing refers to a number of different rituals and practices that are used to exorcise certain entities or energies from a general area.

As I have told you in the last chapter, those that truly wish to pursue the paranormal and to extend the limits of their perception, must be ready to constantly live in a world where the impossible becomes every day. I had used the term 'Chapel Perilous' in this last chapter to speak of a certain state of mind that one encounters when dealing with the supernatural. In the last chapter I told you that there is no possibility of ever freeing yourself from that state of being (this

Perilous state of being), not if you truly wish to explore beyond your current limits.

As a true occult explorer, you must be willing to go far beyond what you now think as possible. I told you that it was better for you to not fall into the trap of the modern agnostic or the Chaos magician, or else you would just find yourself in another cage; one that might be bigger and more varied than the old one but a cage nonetheless.

I also gave you a code of conduct that might help you to be able to deal with this kind of 'being state', this mindset that can be so difficult at times. But I also mentioned that there are different methods to deal with this Chapel perilous, and the best of these methods is to learn proper banishing techniques.

You see, you do not need to constantly fear this chapel perilous, what you need to do is to become comfortable with the fact that there is no more stable ground out there. When you expand your sense perceptions, and when you begin to realize that your perceptions are only the results of beliefs, you can no longer play the game that everyone else is playing. Like the protagonist in the movies, you can no longer go back to your regular life now that you know that vampires are real.

But there are times when you will need your stability. When you will need to at least find a place where you can rest and perhaps forget about the insanity of the world; or was that your insanity?

In order to do this, the best method is to learn how to banish. When you banish in this way, what you are essentially doing is willfully and powerfully taking your attention away from a certain thing. This banishing could be as simple as turning your attention to something else and as complex as creating an actual energetic barrier between you and something else.

Believe it or not, people do banishings all the time. Indeed, it has become quite commonplace to find people doing all sorts of different kinds of banishings. Usually the simplest form is to try to think of the positive instead of the negative; with the advent of the 'law of attraction' and all sorts of new age ideas and movements, this type of banishing has become very common. You essentially turn your attention away from that which brings you down to focusing your attention on something that makes you feel better. Anyone who has ever studied NLP is most likely aware of a number of different forms of banishing's that are practiced by this system.

__Why do we banish?__ Let me explain this again because I want you to really get it. When you extend the abilities of your perception, there will be certain things that you perceive that will be scary or even shocking. Some of these things might be intrusive and depending on your skill *level and expanding paranormal perceptions, they could even be dangerous.*

There will be a time therefore when you wish to rest and to get back to the life that you knew before. We all need a safe haven where we can recharge our batteries so that we can study what we have learnt, contemplate where we wish to go from here, and to gather the impetus needed to go even deeper if we desire.

The only way to achieve this without permanently stopping the advancements that you have already made is to banish those things that create too much chaos within your psyche, for a while. This is the case because a banishing curves the focus of your attention without you having to create a permanent new belief system that might thwart your current abilities. A banishing is an action, either mental, physical, or both, that allows you to create a barrier between you and a perceived entity or object without the need to change your beliefs. For example, you could create an energetic barrier so that a certain ghost or poltergeist might not be able to affect you, without the need to completely rearrange your belief system.

Many paranormal investigators do the opposite of a banishing whenever they face something that causes great fear within them; what they do is reject the existence of these phantasms by repeating almost subconsciously to themselves that what they saw or heard isn't real and, in this way, protect themselves from psychological fear and trauma. When the going gets tough and things really do go bump in the night, the average person starts telling him or herself over and over again that what they are experiencing is not real. They desperately try to re-establish the belief within themselves that ghosts are not real, so that they can feel safe again.

Through different banishing exercises, you can regain control over yourself and your perceptions without the need to create limiting beliefs. You can practice a routine that will allow you to relax and recharge without rejecting that which you are supposedly trying to discover in the first place.

Let us begin then by covering one of the first and perhaps the easiest method of banishing:

Let's say for example that you have been extending your perceptual abilities so that you can see disembodied entities such as ghosts. Let's say that after having gone to a paranormal area, you have arrived at your home and now desire some much-needed rest, but you are not able to find this rest because you keep seeing ghosts or related paranormal activity everywhere. Believe it or not this is a common occurrence for ghost hunters; it seems that many ghosts tend to get curious and follow the unwary ghost hunter home.

When this is the case, you can do a simple banishing that is often times quite helpful. While in bed, or wherever it is that you wish to rest, imagine that you are covered in a beautiful white light. Using your imagination in order to perceive this angelic white light all around you, you will perform the two essential functions of any good banishing:

- You will change your perceptions through the refocusing of your attention.

- You will create an energetic barrier, the strength of which is solely dependent on the power of your attention, which should help to keep away any external influence.

If this banishing is successful, you should be able to have your rest. If done correctly, you will not need to worry about being bothered by these external perceptions that you were having and you should also be free of any external influence that might be negative to you.

Since this is the basis for most good banishing's, I will go into the basic ideas of how this works and give you a real solid methodology so that you can extend the power of this type of banishing.

OUR FATHER THE SUN BANISHING

Here is a better version of the white light banishing that is mentioned above:

In order to do it, close your eyes and relax in that comfortable place where you wish to rest.

- *With your eyes closed imagine a gorgeous white glowing sphere above you. As you concentrate more and more on this gorgeous white sphere of light, you become aware of the fact that it is actually the sun high above. Look into the Sun without the fear of it burning you or destroying your eyes, and feel the power of its light raining down upon you.*

- *With your eyes still closed, imagine that you are lifting off from the ground and flying closer and closer to this giant white Sun. As you get closer the Sun becomes larger and larger and the light that shines upon you become stronger and stronger.*

- *Imagine yourself now being almost upon this light so that it takes up your entire field of vision. Keep traveling towards this gigantic white Sun until you're completely enveloped within it.*

- *Imagine yourself inside this gigantic white Sun, completely covered in this glowing*

> *angelic white light. This light does not burn you but purifies you and invades every single atom of your being. Try to stay within this white angelic world for as long as you can.*
>
> - *When you finally open your eyes you realize that you are back in your body but that because of your journey to this white sun, you are now glowing with power and white angelic energy.*
>
> *Furthermore, you notice that this gorgeous white Sun is still above you and continues to rain down this white angelic light upon you, which cleanses you and keeps you safe, enveloped within a cocoon of white protective light.*

When you do any exercise like the one mentioned above. What you need to do is to involve every single one of your senses into your visualization. This is most important because it is the strength of this visualization which will provide the power required to make this banishing successful.

By using all your senses in your visualization, you will not just be imagining something in your mind's eye, you will actually be living and participating in a completely different reality. You must take a progressive course to make this visualization as real as possible, so real that it actually becomes, if possible, as real as physical reality. There is a progressive nature to this type of visualization and it goes as follows:

- First, as you close your eyes and just imagine this white light around you, what essentially happens is that you see a picture of yourself covered in the white light. If you see a picture of yourself covered in the white light, then you are in a disassociate state[15] when you are picturing this. The first step in enhancing your visualization is to go from a dissociative state to an associative one. To do this what you need to do is to go from imagining a picture of yourself covered by a white light to visualizing yourself as actually being inside the visualization covered by white light; essentially you go from being someone who's looking at a picture, to being someone who is actually in that picture. When you are someone who is looking at a picture, sort of like an audience member looking at a movie, you are in dissociative state. When you become part of that movie so that you visualize yourself actually being one of the people in the picture, you attain an associative state. Being in an Associative state is the first depth to enhancing your visualization.

---

[15] Think of *dissociative state* as you watching a picture of yourself on a TV screen while *associative state* as you participating within your visualization sort of like being in a Star Trek Holodeck.

- When we visualize something in our minds eye, we sometimes see this visualization as being far away. Other times we see this visualization as being kind of cloudy or murky, perhaps we even see this visualization only in black and white. In order to enhance your visualization to the next level, you need to enlarge this visualization within your mind's eye so it covers everything; you are essentially within it and begin to truly feel that you are part of this visualization. Secondly you need to add color and vividness to it. The more color you add to it, the more vivid that it becomes within your mind, the stronger that the visualization will be.

- After you have fully developed the visual aspect of this visualization within your mind's eye, you need to bring in your other senses. Start by visualizing what it would feel like to be covered in this white light. You could for example think of this feeling as being like a light heat upon you, warming up the skin of your entire body. You might want to imagine that this light is actually a type of vibration that begins to give you a tingling feeling all over your body as it envelops it. This is an external feeling. You will also need to work with your internal feelings. Visualize that this light brings a feeling of goodness within the very center of your being. Visualize the feeling that this light washes you completely clean and perhaps creates this wonderful light and happy feeling within you. Imagine that this light makes you feel refreshed, clean, and wonderful. These are internal feelings.

- Begin to visualize that you hear a sound. As this white light envelops you, you might begin to hear a low drone, and as you go closer and closer to this light, this drone becomes louder and louder. You might want to visualize that this drone goes up in pitch so that it not only grows louder but it gets higher and higher in pitch. And as this drone gets louder and higher in pitch, it increases in energy and power.

- If you're very good visualizer, you might even want to experiment with smells or with taste. It is up to you to decide how far you wish to go but the farther that you go to involve all of your senses in your visualization, the stronger that this visualization will become.

- Finally put all of these things together; you are in an associative state, where the visualization that you have completely envelops you and you are part of it. This visualization is very bright and clear and full of color and vividness. You can feel the slight warming and vibrating of your entire body as this light courses through every atom of your being, it makes you feel clean and full of joy. As this light grows in intensity a low drone begins to assail you and this drone gets higher and higher in pitch and grows louder and louder as the light increases in power. You are now completely covered within this protective white light and this reality is as powerful and as real as any reality you have ever experienced.

Try this visualization now and begin to add those different aspects of it until you fully engage all your senses while you are visualizing. You will see for yourself how much your visualizations increase in power. If you practice this technique, engaging your visualized senses in this way, your visualizations will eventually become so strong that there will be little difference between them and what you are experiencing and the 'real' world.

Here I'm also going to give you another banishing ritual that involves light and physical action. Combining physical action with visualized intention greatly increases the power of the banishing; the vanishing becomes supercharged. This banishing was developed by a Chaos magician called Peter Carroll and presented in his book "Liber Kaos":

The Gnostic Pentagram Ritual begins with a visualization of radiance in five areas of the body. Each visualization is assisted by a vibration of one of the bowel sounds I, E, A, O, U. These sounds are vibrated loudly and each a sustained for an entire slow exhalation. Each should produce a physical sensation in the parts of the body to which it is attributed. In effect the body is being played like a musical instrument with each part resonating in sympathy to a particular tone.

Subsequently, pentagrams are drawn in the air at four points around the operator. The pentagrams are drawn and an anti-clockwise quarter turn of the whole body is executed after each pentagram thus returning the body to its original position. The pentagram should be strongly visualized with the eyes opened or closed as desired. Each should be accompanied by a loud intimation fall five vowel sounds I, E, A, O, U in a single exhalation, with one bar of the pentagram being drawn for each sound the IEAOU mantra is used here largely to block discursive thought. Finally, the opening sequence in which the visualization of radiance in various areas of the body, reinforced by the individual I, E, A, O, U mantras, is repeated.

The techniques employed in the ritual are: mantra of vibration, visualization assisted by gesture, breath control.

The ritual entails the visualization of images of radiance within specific areas of the body. These areas correspond with the bodily chakras of some Oriental traditions but not others.

Ritual procedure:

Stand facing any preferred direction.

1. Inhale fully. Exhale slowly sustaining the sound "I" (eehhhhhhh! Like t*ee*th) While visualizing irradiance of energy in the head area.
2. Inhale fully. Exhale slowly sustaining the sound "E" (ehhhhh! Like *e*lf) while visualizing irradiance of energy in the throat area.
3. Inhale fully. Exhale slowly sustaining the sound "A" (ahhhhh! Like *a*nt) while visualizing irradiance of energy in the heart and lungs, which spreads to the muscles of the arms.
4. As in two, but the sound "O" (ohhhh! Like *o*pen) in the belly area.
5. As in two, but the sound "U" (uhhh! Like f*oo*l) in the genital/anal area.
6. Repeats step 5. Then 4, 3, 2, 1, working towards the head.
7. Inhale fully. Exhale slowly, forming each of the IEAOU sounds in turn while, with the left arm, drawing in the air a pentagram, which is also visualized strongly.
8. Make a quarter turn to the left and repeat eight, then continue to turn and draw the remaining pentagrams with the mantra and visualization until returning to the start position.

Perhaps the greatest form of banishing is to be able to 'engage' in a routine that is all encompassing and allows you to focus on it completely.

For me for example, watching television is a wonderful banishing routine. If I ever find that something has just become too much for me at the moment or perhaps I am playing the waiting game and in the meantime I need to stay calm and relaxed, I will put on a good program and watch television for a while.

As long as you can engage in this routine wholeheartedly, you will have created a very powerful banishing indeed.

Banishing's of this type are usually routines that we often consider wastes of time. For example, it might be that many who are reading this book would find playing a videogame to be a great banishing routine for them if they are really avid videogame players. The trick to this banishing like all the others is that you must focus all your attention on it. If there is a routine like this that you find quite pleasurable and at the same time can engage your full attention, then make sure that you take advantage of this routine and use it when you need it.

99% of the stuff that you will perceive 'out there' will be of the kind that can be successfully banished by just turning your attention away from it. This, believe it or not, includes most entity type phenomena which can sometimes seem so invasive. The reason for this is that even if this phenomenon has an exterior nature, that is, it is an actual entity outside of your own psyche, it usually requires your emotional energy to give it power. If you focus your attention completely on other matters then this entity has no more power and can therefore do little to affect your reality.

It is quite possible for example to have ghouls running through your house while you are merrily playing a good videogame, watching a great movie, or reading some great book that you were meaning to check out. That is those entities might be there to one extent or another, there might even be small physical effects because of these entities, but without hardly any of your attention, after a while, these entities will either move away or become completely inert. No worries as these entities will soon move away as soon as they perceive some kind of useful emotional energy elsewhere.

Save this wonderful routine therefore, save this vice, so that you can use it as a balm whenever you need to relax.

The final banishing that I'm going to mention should be used if you ever find yourself, or someone that you know, lost in a different reality structure. There are times, for example when after long periods of hypnagogic exercises, when you might have a very difficult time engaging in your present physical reality. While this is not often a dangerous thing, and a good nap is usually the best cure, there are times when you need to get into the here and now quickly.

Like they say, you should not operate a vehicle while taking this medicine.

When you begin to expand your perceptions, you begin to expand your psyche. Sometimes these expansions can be quite mind-bending and you could even say aggressive depending on how much they get a hold of you. When this is the case and you need to engage in 'reality', you will need to do this banishing as a last safe measure.

There are times when you will need to take a nice cold shower.

If you ever need to engage in regular life but you seem to be lost in an almost dreamlike state, which comes from expanding your paranormal abilities, you need to take a quick cold shower to get back to the physical plane. A nice cold shower will wake you up and no matter how deep you are into an altered state, the cold water hitting your body will instantly put you back in this physical plane. Once comfortably in this physical plane, this concrete vanilla reality, you can usually stay here as long as you want. If the dissociative state continues, then get back into that shower until you feel like yourself again. Make sure that you have a warm meal or a good cup of coffee when you get out.

These banishing's will allow you to deal with Chapel perilous. They are not meant to put up a permanent wall between you and the chaos 'out there'. They are to be used to provide an energizing cocoon when you need to take a break from it all. Nobody can be on the go all the time and to do so would indeed trap you in foreign mental structures perhaps permanently.

To bring yourself back to 'reality' by creating a whole new belief system where you think that everything out there is just the belief that you can play with, is not good enough because it will just create a wall between you and the real Weirdness out there. This is the ultimate banishing because it creates a true wall between you and those things that you were trying to perceive; the occult, the supernatural, the paranormal, the chaos of the dark sea of perception.

Banishing then does not become a way of separating yourself from the infinite out there, because there is no possibility of your separation from it. What it does is it allows you to control your space in these belief structures so that you can begin to explore them all fully, realizing that they're all true and as concrete and real as the consensual world we all consider to be so solid.

EPILOGUE

So, what are we left with when all is said and done?

I have given you some methodology in order to expand your sensual and intuitive capabilities. This methodology is quite powerful and if you follow it with enough discipline, you will get a real good look behind the curtain. The curtain is imposed on us and we impose it upon ourselves; it is a very big, thick, and heavy curtain but it can be moved aside with some effort.

Paranormal research has increased to a great degree in the last few years, unfortunately the quality of this research has not improved. Some might say that because of the large number of weekend warrior type researchers, paranormal research has actually gone down in quality and daring. It might be the case that some of this research has lost its edge due to the amount of people engaging in it in recent years but it is also my belief that this research has gone down in quality because we have hit a type of impasse here in the West. This impasse is due to the fact that there's only so far that science can take us using its current belief structure. Now when I speak of science here I am not talking about true scientific method but about those entrenched beliefs that maintain a type of orderly religiosity over human possibility and perception.

It might seem that I am picking a lot on the scientific establishment. In actuality I'm not picking on science itself but on those that would use its findings to create a new type of religion that can only restrict man and his greater potential. I think of our, still emerging, science as a very powerful way to expand our power in this universe. Unfortunately, this power is coveted and used by those that would like to increase their personal power at the cost of others. Those that would selfishly increase their power in this way, are not interested in the greater power of the whole but in creating greater power for themselves at the cost of everyone else. It is the same selfish power grab that created a Christian church which was more interested in gaining wealth and controlling the masses than in pursuing communion with God.

A true scientist does not define something as an ultimate truth and does not rely on a bureaucratic system to maintain these supposed truths. A true scientist is someone who quests for knowledge and uses empirical methodology deeply steeped in logic. While it might be possible that we can ultimately find general truths about our universe, these truths will never be discovered until scientists, paranormal researchers, and any other person who quests for the unknown, is able to completely remove the blinders created by social indoctrination. Scientists have not done this yet, paranormal researchers have not done this yet either, and the average person is not willing to do this because they're far too comfortable in their everyday lives. Instrumentation cannot do this because instrumentation is created to see what the creator wishes to see.

But can there be a new science? Perhaps that is what this new century will be all about. Perhaps someday we will be able to combine our incredible technological advances with our totally untapped perceptual potentials. The 'old schools' managed to attain great knowledge simply through the use of experimentation with psychotropic flora and fauna. Perhaps the great advances that we are making in pharmacology might allow us to do this as well. I personally trust that if we truly commit ourselves in the proper way, we can greatly increase the knowledge that we have attained, and that our ancestors attained through their methods. I have faith in scientific principles; my problem is not with the principles itself but with those that would turn those principles into religious dogma.

Expansion, using the methods described in this book, is an asset. The ancient schools of which I speak became incredibly powerful because the individuals within them practiced these methods. With greater perceptual capability you begin to see that which others cannot. In a way it allows you to be a step ahead of the competition and this can be an invaluable asset.

Expanding your awareness is an incredibly important aspect of intelligence. Everything in this book, especially in the earlier chapters, will allow you to begin to see things from a different perspective. This perspective will give you a great boost intellectually since intellectual expansion is only possible when we are able to expand the way in which we can perceive and define the things around us. The more that you can see things from different angles the smarter that you will become.

Auric perception will allow you to perceive truth or falsehood. It will allow you to perceive another's health and even another's potential. It will allow you to begin to perceive intention and in this way it will allow you to perceive their future. Most UFO phenomenon, ghosts, poltergeists, big-foot, and other cryptic phenomenon, can be located, tracked, and identified by someone adept in this methodology. Your natural visual receptors therefore will be of a far greater use to you than any current instruments; like electromagnetic meters, thermal imaging devices, and video cameras with current optic enhancements.

Expanding your subconscious allows you to expand your possibilities. Any creation begins in the subconscious and then is expressed in what we consider to be reality. Understanding your subconscious, you will understand the forces that are shaping your reality. Learning to deal with these forces will allow you to create with far greater facility than those that would plow headlong into something thinking that it's all about charts, measures, hard work, and 12 hour days.

It is my great wish that you expand on all the ideas presented here and that you find your own methodologies as you go along. It is also my hope that you are encouraged to create groups and organizations that can use empirical methodology to explore what has hitherto been referred to as the occult, the paranormal, the supernatural, the Weird, the far too strange to be taken seriously.

FURTHER READING

While you might find these books harder to find because they are all older books, they do represent a good foundation of knowledge that applies directly to the book I have written. I particularly recommend the books marked with an asterisk.

Cosmic Trigger Trilogy by Robert Anton Wilson

Prometheus Rising by Robert Anton Wilson

Liber Kaos by Peter J. Carroll

Prime Chaos by Phil Hine

The Nature of Personal Reality: Specific, Practical Techniques for Solving Everyday Problems and Enriching the Life You Know* by Jane Roberts

Tales of Power* by Carlos Castaneda

Using Your Brain For a Change: Neuro-Linguistic Programming by Richard Bandler

Path Notes of an American Ninja Master by Glenn Morris

The Mothman Prophecies by John A. Keel

I hope you enjoyed this book.

If you would like to receive occasional emails when I release new books and interesting information, you can join my private mailing list.

johnkreiter.com/mailing-list-sign-up

For questions and comments, you can reach me though my site at
http://johnkreiter.com/the-book-that-shows-you-how-to-get-proof-of-the-paranormal/

Or though Facebook at
facebook.com/johnkreiterdotcom

Thank you for reading.

Printed in Great Britain
by Amazon